Cambridge Elements ≡

Elements in Translation and Interpreting
edited by
Kirsten Malmkjær
University of Leicester
Sabine Braun
University of Surrey

TRANSLATION AND GENRE

B. J. Woodstein
University of East Anglia

CAMBRIDGE
UNIVERSITY PRESS

CAMBRIDGE
UNIVERSITY PRESS

University Printing House, Cambridge CB2 8BS, United Kingdom

One Liberty Plaza, 20th Floor, New York, NY 10006, USA

477 Williamstown Road, Port Melbourne, VIC 3207, Australia

314–321, 3rd Floor, Plot 3, Splendor Forum, Jasola District Centre,
New Delhi – 110025, India

103 Penang Road, #05–06/07, Visioncrest Commercial, Singapore 238467

Cambridge University Press is part of the University of Cambridge.

It furthers the University's mission by disseminating knowledge in the pursuit of
education, learning, and research at the highest international levels of excellence.

www.cambridge.org
Information on this title: www.cambridge.org/9781108926331
DOI: 10.1017/9781108923255

First published 2022

A catalogue record for this publication is available from the British Library.

ISBN 978-1-108-92633-1 Paperback
ISSN 2633-6480 (online)
ISSN 2633-6472 (print)

Translation and Genre

Elements in Translation and Interpreting

DOI:10.1017/9781108923255
First published online: July 2022

B. J. Woodstein
University of East Anglia

Author for correspondence: B. J. Woodstein, b.epstein@uea.ac.uk

Abstract: What is a genre? How do genres differ between cultures and languages? How do generic texts get translated and how does the specific genre affect the act of translation? This Element surveys the concept of genre itself, a number of different genres and what happens to these genres through translation, while also providing an overview of research on these topics along with research-based approaches for translating work that can perhaps be labelled as generic.

Keywords: translation, genre, science fiction, children's literature, literature, drama, women's fiction, and queer literature

ISBNs: 9781108926331 (PB), 9781108923255 (OC)
ISSNs: 2633-6480 (online), 2633-6472 (print)

Contents

Introduction

What is a genre? How do genres differ between cultures and languages? What is the connection between genre and style and text type? How do generic texts get translated and how does the specific genre affect the act of translation, if it does? This Element surveys the concept of genre itself, analyses a number of different genres and explores what happens to these genres through translation, while also providing an overview of research on these topics along with approaches for translating work that can perhaps be labelled as generic.

The first section of this Element will explore genre in general, looking at the concept and its influence on how people write, translate, market and read books. In that section, I will begin to refer to the translation of generic texts in a broad sense and then, following the initial section, I turn more specifically to translation. To do this, I focus on six different genres; space limitations preclude me from exploring every possible genre, even if I thought that would be a useful thing to do, but in fact I think looking at a few example text types is fascinating in itself and also proves the overall point that genres are much more complicated than generally assumed. Here, I analyse women's writing, drama, LGBTQ+ literature, crime fiction, children's literature and science fiction as genres and then I discuss the challenges inherent in translating them and approaches to doing so. I could just as easily have chosen a different set of genres, so I acknowledge the limited and subjective nature of this particular analysis from the outset. In each section, I attempt to define the genre, or at least understand its key characteristics, and then to discuss its translation. Finally, I end the Element by deconstructing and critiquing genre, reframing it as a set of expectations. I conclude that although there are uses for generic labels and categories, they can also be limiting and can restrict authors, translators and readers, among others. While I explore research-based suggestions for specific translational challenges, some of which are inherent to a given genre in both the source and target cultures, there is also a clear understanding that translators must be allowed to be as flexible and creative as the original writers in order to carry out their work.

My own scholarly interest in genre began many years ago when I was asked to take over an MA class in literary translation that focussed on the translation of generic texts. I started to teach the course in the middle of the term because the previous lecturer retired then and so I had to use the already existing syllabus. To my surprise, the syllabus included weeks on topics such as women's fiction and children's literature; I had assumed that women could write work in any genre and that books by women did not comprise their own genre purely by dint of the gender of the authors, and I had likewise thought that works for children could encompass all genres. But I quickly discovered that many of the students disagreed with me; they wanted to have handy labels for understanding texts so that they could then – so they thought – know exactly how to translate these works. Surely, they argued, 'chick lit' would be translated very differently from a picture book. I did not disagree with this entirely, but I was also concerned that this view was limiting. I wanted to take each text on its own terms, and sometimes this includes issues of genre as one of the foremost concerns and sometimes it does not. Since that first class, I have now spent over a dozen years teaching and thinking about translating genre, and more time than that as a translator of many texts in a wide range of genres or styles. This has led me to argue that the idea of genre is both beneficial and detrimental when it comes to studying and carrying out translation, and I seek to encourage people to understand and dismantle genre. Writing or translating within – or without – a genre can perhaps make a translator's work easier, but doing so can also be activist and can challenge people's ideas about literature, language or society. In other words, use it or disregard it as needed for each particular translation task.

Luise von Flotow notes, 'Translation makes deliberate choices about which writer to translate, which foreign ideas and materials to disseminate. These choices are premeditated, planned and carefully evaluated, and the meticulous word-by-word labour of translation is often equally self-aware. In other words, translation, it can be argued, is as intentional, as activist, as deliberate as any feminist or otherwise socially-activist activity' (2011, p. 4). If genres are understood in a particular way in particular cultures, then editors must make a choice about which text to have translated and why, and then translators make translatorial choices as they work, and such choices – which may be activist – can influence how a text is received, including what genre it is perceived as belonging to. This suggests that translators must be aware of genre definitions in both the source and target cultures and would ideally have knowledge and experience with a range of genres as well as with strategies for translating those genres. This, then, is what I hope to explore in what follows.

Defining Genre

Humans find labels and categories comforting. There is an evolutionary basis here, in that in our distant past, we would have needed to know who was 'us' and who was 'them', what was safe to eat and what was poisonous, which animals were friendly and which were dangerous, and so forth (e.g. Henderson 2018 or Moffett 2013, pp. 223–4). Today, we continue to categorise; it can lead to stereotyping and to getting things wrong, but it can also serve as a form of shorthand that helps us quickly figure out what we need to do in a particular situation. Labels, including generic ones, communicate information to us.

The word 'genre' itself is a confusing one. As Anis S. Bawarshi and Mary Jo Reiff write, the lack of clarity around the term stems from its etymology,

> 'which is borrowed from French. On the one hand, *genre* can be traced, through its related word *gender*, to the Latin word *genus*, which refers to "kind" or "a class of things." On the other hand, *genre*, again through its related word *gender*, can be traced to the Latin cognate *gener*, meaning to generate. The range of ways genre has been defined and used throughout its history reflects its etymology' (2010, pp. 3–4, emphasis in original).

So a genre is both a label for a kind of thing but also can generate or create the thing in and of itself; it can be viewed as creative, re-creative (and perhaps recreational) and constrictive, all at once.

Wai Chee Dimock asks,

> 'What exactly are genres? Are they a classifying system matching the phenomenal world of objects, a sorting principle that separates oranges from apples? Or are they less than that, a taxonomy that never fully taxono-mizes, labels that never quite keep things straight? What archives come with genres, what critical lexicons do they offer, and what maps do they yield? And how does the rise of digitization change these archives, lexicons, and maps?' (2007, p. 1377).

Not all these questions can be answered in this Element, but they are a useful point of departure.

A possible introductory definition of genre in terms of literature is that it is a way to categorise groups: '[a] particular genre category refers to the way the individual fictions which belong to it can be grouped together in terms of similar plots, stereotypes, settings, themes, style, emotional affects, and so on . . . such categories function as important guides to our viewing choices and practices' (Gledhill and Ball, 1997/2013, p. 347). In other words, similarities of style or subject or features can group certain texts together. One might then wonder how many similarities two or more texts need to share before they are placed together and whether there is a hierarchy of commonalities, with some given more precedence than others.

Genre is not the only word employed to describe this sort of concept, of course. Some critics, such as Christiane Nord, use the term text type instead or interchangeably with the term genre (1988, p. 21), whereas I would consider text type to be broader and genre to be more specific; text types may be linked to the function of the text. Katharina Reiß, quoted by Jeremy Munday, also refers to text type as the larger category and then 'text varieties or genres' as smaller groupings within the categories (2008, p. 72). Andrew Bennett and Nicholas Royle define genre as 'a kind; a literary type or style' (2014, p. 322). This complicates things further, conflating genre both with type and with style. Jean Boase-Beier defines style as the form of expression (2019, p. 4), while Bennett and Royle seem to suggest that each author has their own 'distinctive' style (2014, p. 93). Citing Gilles Deleuze, they further discuss style as a 'sort of signature or singularity in terms of the invention of a new kind of language, a kind of foreign language within a language' (2014, p. 94). Considering that genre as a whole seems to bring various texts together under a common umbrella, style, at least according to these definitions, would appear to separate them, focussing on the uniqueness of each author's work or each text, unless one argues that each genre has its own specific style. Other possible terms used alongside or instead of genre include category or system or mode. Given such diffuse definitions, then, I here claim that text type is the largest, broadest category, followed by genres within those various types, and then each text or each individual author may have their own style, regardless of whether they are writing in or categorised as belonging to a particular genre or not. There is some overlap, so, for instance, a number of texts within a given genre may have certain commonalities of style, but despite this, I would suggest that style is a more specific marker.

To return, then, to types of genre, Stephen Owen notes that many still subscribe to Hegel's scheme of three 'core genres, epic (narrative), lyric, and dramatic, which correspond to situations of discourse – speaking about an other, speaking for oneself, speaking as an other' (2007, p. 1391; cf. Bawarshi and Reiff on this so-called neoclassical taxonomical system, 2010, pp. 15–16). But this is a very Western view, as Owen goes on to note: 'If those three core genres coincide with a primary map of literary genres only in the European literary tradition, this coincidence may be seen either as one local construction among many or as the result of Europe's unique capacity to discover and ground genre in a higher conceptual order' (2007, p. 1391). Bawarshi and Reiff go on to cite Northrop Frye, who lists four archetypical genres or formats – 'comedy, romance, tragedy, and irony/satire' – and even links each one to a different season (2010, p. 16).

Meanwhile, Bennett and Royle offer this list of genres: 'Poetry, drama, novel may be subdivided into lyric (including elegy, ode, song, sonnet, etc.), the epic, tragedy, comedy, short story, biography, etc.' (2014, p. 322). This list continues to be quite focussed on classic forms that may or may not exist in every culture. Examples of typical genres in English might include horror, humour or comedy, fantasy, crime/mystery, science fiction, romance, realistic literature, historical, Christian fiction and much more. Others might have even more specific lists;

John Frow cites scholars who, for example, differentiate between 'sensuous contemporaries' and 'sweet contemporaries' or between 'women's fiction' and 'chick lit' (2006, p. 139). It is obvious from the varying lists of genre categories that history, culture, language and literary tradition will influence which genre headings are recognised, and which ones are considered important or even canonical. Each literary system, including genres, is distinct.

Furthermore, how texts or authors are sorted into genres is debatable, too. Depending on the circumstances, it could be the author, the publisher, the audience, critics, booksellers or others who decide the supposed genre. Nord notes that literary genres 'are often differentiated by special features of subject matter of content ... extension [length] ... or by their affiliation to a literary era ... as well as by certain stylistic properties' (1988, pp. 21–2). While this is true, this connects to a much larger concept. One of the key aspects of genre is that it shapes both writer and reader expectations (and thus, in turn, it influences how translators translate). If someone picks up, for example, a romance novel or a science fiction work, they will have certain ideas in mind about the style, substance and structure of the work. If their expectations are not met, they might find this stimulating and exciting, or they might choose not to read the book because it is not what they were looking for. Kimberley Reynolds writes that genre literature 'appeals to large groups of readers by promising and providing familiar reading experiences. It tends to do this through abiding by conventions, employing stereotypes, following formulae, and perhaps resorting to clichéd expressions' (2011, p. 78). While I agree with the first part, in that the genre a book belongs to informs readers about what to expect, I believe that what follows in this Element might suggest that the use of formulae and stereotypes is not always to be found in these works, despite the widespread belief that they are. Reynolds, too, acknowledges that 'the constraints of convention can be a spur to innovation, provoking writers to explore the possibilities for simultaneously conforming to and transcending genre expectations' (2011, p. 78). Still, given the importance of audience expectations, genre can sometimes be understood as a marketing tool; the conventions around what a particular format is can impact not only how a book is written and what the subject of the work is but also how the cover or illustrations are designed, the font size and style, the size and shape of the book, where the text is placed in a library or bookstore, how it gets advertised or reviewed, how it is analysed and more.

John Frow writes, 'The work of genre, then, is to mediate between a social situation and the text which realises certain features of this situation, or which responds strategically to its demands. Genre shapes strategies for occasions; it gets a certain kind of work done' (2006, pp. 14–15). In other words, genre could perhaps be understood as the rules of a game; to have a fair and enjoyable game, all the players want and need to know how they are to play. But a genre is far from simply a strict set of guidelines, I would suggest; writers can break the rules, as Reynolds mentions. There are conventions, and yet there is flexibility. Indeed, Frow refers to the 'danger' of being 'rigid' in terms of how much control the concept of genre has (2006, p. 14). But genre is not just a playful game; as Thomas O. Beebee notes, '[t]he ideology of genre is all around us' (1994, p. 4).

Works can fall into multiple genres (a horror story written in graphic format, for example, or a fantastical bildungsroman); Frow notes that a work can be a 'member' of several different categories (2006, p. 27) and quotes Jacques Derrida on how a text can 'participate' in a genre without explicitly 'belonging' to it (2006, p. 27). Naturally, too, there are genres within genres (such as romances that take place in medical settings or psychological thrillers); Frow differentiates between simple and complex genres (2006, p. 33), a distinction I find less useful but that does remind us that genres can contain multitudes. And Dimock, too, notes that besides texts being able to belong to multiple genres or text types, genres are also 'empirical rather than logical . . . and as such likely to be confronted with specimens they are not able to foresee' (2007, p. 1378). Genres are ever-evolving; '[g]enres have solid names, ontologized names. What these names designate, though, is not taxonomic classes of equal solidity but fields at once emerging and ephemeral, defined over and over again by new entries that are still being produced' (Dimock 2007, p. 1379). So we try to define them, knowing that many texts slip across boundaries and that definitions change according to time and place.

And, of course, as noted earlier, genres are different in different cultures and languages; Owen rightfully comments that '[g]enre in history is a sediment of contingencies and changing motives' (2007, p. 1391), and Nord writes that '[g]enre conventions are not universal, but linked to a certain culture at a certain time' (1988, p. 21). A specific example would be cartoons versus manga versus *bande dessinée*, all of which tend to be lumped together as comics or graphic works. Differing views of what might seem like something under the same taxonomical umbrella can impact on how a translator chooses to translate a particular work. For example, in both my own scholarly research and my translation practice, I have found that children's literature is not viewed in the same way in English-speaking countries versus Scandinavian-speaking ones; editors and publishers have said that certain subjects, words or styles of writing are unacceptable or even taboo in one culture, whereas they are not in another. Frow writes that being 'a member of a culture is knowing how' to understand the generic conventions of that culture (2006, p. 56); translators are, by definition, members of at least two cultures.

Genre is also influenced by power. Some genres are considered more important or highbrow than others and are more likely to be respected, published, reviewed, assigned in schools or universities as reading or translated. An author's identity, whether real or perceived, can influence which genre their work is ascribed to and this can impact upon their career and their success. The concept of the 'canon' is about how a very narrow range of texts and authors have been 'monumentalized', as Bennett and Royle phrase it (2009, p. 45); canonical works have generally been by and about white, middle-class, Christian, cisgender, heterosexual, able-bodied people from so-called WEIRD nations (Western, educated, industrialised, rich, developed) (e.g. Bloom 1994). In other words, certain authors, texts or text types are more or less likely to get published in the first place and then translated, and if they are translated, strategies may differ depending on the perception of the genre. This may be something that translators can challenge with their work, or it could be to their benefit, or it might be something that happens to the text but is not relevant to the translator.

Related to the topic of genre is that of *skopos*, or function. This theory suggests that writers, publishers, translators and others involved in the publication of a work should consider why a text has been written, who it is aimed at and why it is being translated (Nord 1997, pp. 27–31). Beebee refers to functions of genres, which he terms 'use-values' (1994, p. 7), when he writes that 'generic differences are grounded in the "use-value" of a discourse rather than in its content, formal features, or its rules of production' (1997, p. 7). That is to say that different genres have different purposes and expect a different type of reaction or interaction from their readership, which in turns anticipates certain features or experiences from the texts. There are perceptions about the functions specific texts types or genres have, for example being educational or informative, bringing pleasure, challenging received notions and so on. Understanding the possible function or functions of an individual text and the genre or genres it belongs to before translating it means considering its production and distribution, the text itself and its reception in both the source and the target languages. The *skopos* may change or be expected to change in translation. Jeremy Munday cites Katharina Reiβ on the four primary text types and their functions: an informative text aims to communicate information; in an expressive text, the 'author or "sender" is foregrounded, as well as the form of the message'; the intention of an operative text 'is to appeal to or persuade the reader or "receiver" of the text to act in a certain way'; and then there are audiomedial works, 'such as films and visual and spoken advertisements which supplement the other three functions with visual images, music, etc.' (2008, p. 72). Perhaps it is clearer to say that there are three main text types in Reiβ's formulation, and they can also include images; children's literature, which will be discussed in the section 'Genre 5', can be considered to belong to one or more of the three types, with the concomitant functions, and also to usually have visual images, which themselves may have the same or different functions. It seems obvious that a text could be informative and expressive and operative all at once, or could have one of those functions in one section and a different one in another, or could combine functions in some other pattern. Reiβ argues that a translator must first analyse the text to determine the text type and then the text variety within that type (1971/2004, p. 173), followed by the style (1971/2004, p. 174), and then can simply carry out what she calls a 'process of reverbaliza-tion' (1971/2004, p. 175). I question, however, whether this is always as simple a matter to determine as Reiβ seems to be implying, and, of course, as already discussed, text types and genres have changed in function and perception over time and continue to change. And how a sender and a receiver – and the receiver here will include the translator – view texts may drastically differ. Munday, too, notes metaphors in informative texts as an example of works that cross type boundaries and also feels that focussing on function ignores the 'translator's own role and purpose, as well as sociocultural pressures' (2008, p. 75). Nonetheless, the aim or function of a given text will certainly be one of many considerations a translator will have to be aware of.

In short, genre is about expectations. It can be beneficial as a label – people have a sense of what they are getting – but it can also be constricting or stereotyping. Authors, and indeed translators, have a right to play around with genre conventions and to bring elements or rules from different genres together. This obviously raises the question of whether genres have any real use, if writers are going to break down the boundaries between them. In addition, if certain strategies are said to be useful for translators of more than one genre or with more than one type of generic element, that challenges the idea of strict distinctions between genres, text types or labels.

The following sections will seek to explore all this, by using several genres in order to explore the expectations of each example genre and the effect of these expectations on writers, translators and readers; we could put this another way by saying that genre categories influence the processes of writing, translating and reading. Frow writes that no work 'is ever unframed ... [t]exts and genres exist in an unstable relationship' (2006, p. 30): so how much instability can we accept? And, furthermore, since translation is necessarily not a literal transfer-ence of the text from one language and culture to another, it creates more instability. Emily Apter writes that '[t]ranslation ... effects a subtle generic shift in how we view the literary text' (2007, p. 1410), which means that a text may not remain within the same genre, or the same understanding of genre, in the target culture. A translator is not only transporting a specific author and text but potentially even a text type or genre; they must understand genres and ideas of genres in both the source and target cultures in order to be able to analyse the texts they are working on and then to translate them.

Genre 1: Women's Writing

Definitions

To start the exploration of genres, I will look at women's writing, in part because, many years ago, I was puzzled by the very concept that it would be considered a genre of its own. I, perhaps wrongly, assumed that writing by women, much like writing by men or writing by people of any other gender, could exist in any genre or combination of genres and that people of all genders might be interested in reading it. Clearly, this is a debate that is still ongoing as, just recently, author Jeanette Winterson complained about people thinking she belonged to the category of 'wimmins fiction' [*sic*], by which she clearly meant something negative, rather than an empowering, proud field that was opposed to 'men's fiction' (Flood 2021a, p. 4). Another author, Joanne Harris, replied angrily, 'Women are neither a genre, nor a single experience' (Flood 2021a, p. 4). So what is women's (or wimmins) writing? And is it a genre?

First of all, the very name of the genre seems to assume that it is writing by women; further assumptions might be that it is about women and for women. This may be a problematic set of assumptions because then one must define the term 'woman', and gender is a social and cultural construct. Additionally, women, like all other groups, are not homogenous, and what may interest a woman who is in a particular culture, from a specific background in regard to class and ethnicity, of a given sexuality and ability, and of a certain age, may not be at all appealing to a woman with differing experiences and characteristics. Carol Maier writes that

> 'unqualified, "woman" is not a reliable, stable point of departure for either the discussion or the practice of translation of work from any genre. On the contrary, one finds repeatedly that neither authors nor characters – and certainly not readers – conform to any fixed understanding of "woman," even though they are defined as women by themselves or others. Perhaps more importantly, one frequently finds that even when "woman" can be used appropriately, to use it as a single form of definition is to exclude other definitions that may be equally or more determinant' (1998, p. 97).

To suggest that all women – whatever women are or might be – must write and/or want to read a certain kind of literature is unreasonable, as Winterson's apparent complaint reveals, because she did not want her writing to be categorised as sharing similarities with a type of work that she seems to disdain (as her misspelling of 'women' suggests, even though some people find that spelling valuable, since it removes the 'man' from the word).

Also, there is no large category called men's writing; there is a smaller field called 'lad lit', which is defined as a 'marketing term of the 1990s in Britain, referring to a new kind of popular fiction concerning the "lad" of that period, a supposedly carefree hedonist devoted to football, beer, music, and casual sex' (Oxford Reference, 2021, n.p.), but this is a very specific subsection of what is generally simply considered to be writing. Nor is there a corresponding category of writing beyond the gender binary, although that may be because it is only quite recently that more people have been open about being neither male nor female and have been using labels such as genderqueer or non-binary. In other words, there is an apparent assumption that writing by men, and presumably about men, is the norm while women's writing is in contrast to the norm and must be given its own genre heading. Culture is not gender-neutral; women's spaces – such as women's magazines or women's sections of the newspaper or women's radio or TV programmes – are named in a way that those aimed at men or at everyone are not (e.g. Gledhill and Ball 1997/2013, p. 341). This implies that writing by and about men should be of interest to anyone, while writing by and about women would only be of interest to women (despite the aforementioned issue of women not all being the same or having the same literary enthusiasms).

Of course it must be acknowledged that women were long kept from being fully equal and active citizens in many societies, including here in the West, where I am writing from. Previously, I mentioned the idea of the canon, and the literary canon has seldom included women. As Lillian S. Robinson notes,

> 'a gentleman is inescapably – that is, by definition – a member of a privileged class and of the male sex. From this perspective, it is probably quite accurate to think of the canon as an entirely gentlemanly artifact, considering how few works by non-members of that class and sex make it into the informal agglomeration of course syllabi, anthologies, and widely-commented upon "standard authors" that constitutes the canon as it is generally understood'
> (1983, p. 84).

Women may have written privately but could not necessarily get published or have their work reach large audiences in the way men could (e.g. see Virginia Woolf's essay on how literature has traditionally been a male space, imbued with male values 1929/2008); for this reason, it is important to highlight works written by women and to discuss the specific circumstances around their writing. This is a strong reason for differentiating women's writing as its own category; raising awareness of a (heterogeneous) group of people who have frequently been made invisible or not allowed to participate in politics and culture is very important. And yet, this might also be an issue because labelling women's writing as being by and/or about and/or for women may mean that men do not read such works. For example, M. A. Sieghart carried out research that showed that only 19 per cent of the readers of bestselling books by women are male, whereas men comprise 55 per cent of the readers of bestselling books by men; it seems that men are more likely to read a book by a man and only by a woman if the female author is identified by initials, rather than by a (feminine) first name, and if they thereby did not know the author was female (2021, p. 25). So women's writing may get published today, but the readership is likely to be women only, further differentiating it from standard or norm literature.

But given that women's writing is defined in part as being different from the norm, what else is it exactly? Christine Gledhill and Vicky Ball, writing about soap opera, describe it this way:

> 'Women's genres, such as women's fiction and soap opera, draw on a tradition of domestic realism in which a set of highly articulate discursive forms – talk, the confessional heart-to-heart, gossip – work through psychic and social contradictions which melodrama must externalize through expressive action. Far from representing an "excess" of emotion which displaces action, talk in soap opera *is* its action, while action in masculine genres more often than not represents unexpressed and often inexpressible male emotion, which needs a melodramatic climax to break out' (1997/2013, p. 378, emphasis in original).

That is to say, they seem to define women's genres, including women's fiction, as being talk-based and as focussing heavily on emotions. Other articles, panels and discussions likewise seem to consider women's fiction as being about 'emotion', while in contrast, literature by and for men is supposedly about the 'containment of emotion and feeling' (Galo 2016, n.p.), although not all authors or readers would agree with this, regardless of gender. It is certainly rather stereotyped to suggest that women have feelings and men do not or that women are interested in exploring emotions, while men are not.

Other scholars suggest a wider range of subjects for women's writing, depending on where and when it was produced; for example, 'early American novels [by women] showed the restrictions of women's lives but entered into a debate about women's status and rights, particularly as it concerned female education' (Swedberg 2021, n.p.), while some other women's writing is thought to focus on women's search for identity (Gardiner 1981, p. 347), and the subcategory of 'chick lit' is about young women's lives in particular and perhaps especially about them as sexual beings (Feral 2011, p. 183). There are other subcategories of women's writing, which have their own subjects and style. A typical example is romance, which is the 'top-grossing genre in the

North American publishing industry' and yet 'one of the most reviled' (Wood 2015, p. 293) and of course contains many subgenres of its own, such as paranormal or historical or spiritual. Romances are said to have 'a central love story and an emotionally satisfying and optimistic ending' (RWA n.d., n. p.) and to have 'something meaningful to say about women's experiences in culture' (Wood 2015, p. 293), while others suggest that perhaps they are 'patriarchal' in their view or maybe they offer women the nurturing women crave and do not receive (Beebee 1994, p. 6). On the whole, though,

> '[f]eminist literary criticism has argued that our understanding of literary para-
> digms, metaphors, and meaning in general is profoundly affected by the gender
> of both author and audience. Critics from this school posit that a woman's
> experience comprises unique perceptions and emotions, and that women and
> men do not inhabit an identical world, or at the very least do not view it
> identically, in that sexual difference as a social construct has implications for
> how one interprets as well as how one is interpreted' (Henitiuk, 1999, p. 469).

Clearly, then, it seems that there is a general belief that women's writing is by and about women and that it is in some way about women's lives, selves, emotions and experiences. Whether this very broad definition is enough to make it its own genre is, I would suggest, debatable. It also ignores the important idea of inter-sectionality, or the connections, in this case, between a person's gender identity and their sexuality, ethnicity, religion, (dis)ability, class, location, level of education and so forth. Women are not just one thing; every woman will have their own experiences, and it is hard to claim that a work by or about a woman should somehow speak to all women readers. Furthermore, I am personally unconvinced that such writing should primarily be considered to be aimed at women readers because it strikes me as being of universal interest and importance.

Translation

Having come up with a rather vague and quite problematic definition for the genre of women's writing, I wish to now turn to the specific issue of translating it. If women's writing is its own field, then is there a particular way of translating it that differs from how a translator might translate, for example, poetry by a male writer?

Olga Castro and Emek Ergun write,

> '"Feminist translation" is often introduced to describe the theories and
> practices developed in bilingual Quebec, Canada, by a group of translators
> and translation scholars in the 1970s and 1980s. The Canadians were indeed
> first in openly claiming the label "feminist translation" to describe their
> efforts to incorporate feminist values into their avant-garde literary

translation projects and enable new ways of articulation to subvert and unsettle the patriarchal language' (2018, p. 126).

However, Castro and Ergun state that although some important work came out of Canada, some of which is explored later in this Element,

'many cases of feminist approaches to translation date back centuries .... Reconceived in this way, feminist translation encompasses not only politically engaged textual translation strategies ... but also any form of discursive political intervention made in various processes of translation in pursuit of gender justice – e.g. the strategic use of translation as an apparatus of cross-border dialogue to disseminate feminist ideas and build transnational feminist solidarities. Elaborating the history of feminist translation in such a geohistorically expansive context is urgently needed to reveal that the interaction between gender politics and translation politics is not a recent trend' (2018, p. 126).

Castro and Ergun go on to show examples of such feminist methods, including adding female characters, writing a feminist introduction to the translation, using pseudonyms for translation work, making texts non-sexist and so on (2018, p. 127).

Although those historical examples exist, it is also undeniable that the Canadian school has been important. Castro and Ergun explain that the foundations of the Canadian scholars' and translators' work were 'informed by a politics of identity that linked sexual difference (and the alienation of women in the phallocentric language) to cultural difference (the hegemonic status of Anglo values in franco-phone Quebec)' (2018, p. 128). Luise von Flotow, who is one of the prominent scholars in this area, notes that people have been thinking and writing about the translation of women's writing at least since the 1990s, notwithstanding the chal-lenges involved in trying to describe an unwieldy category that is far from uniform in its styles and subjects (2011, p. 1). She describes the early work in this way:

'Identity politics underlie most of this writing, and in the area of translation, this produced theoretical work engaging directly with power differentials that rule relations between the sexes, within society, and between cultures, and that are often revealed in the detailed study of translated literatures. These issues include censorship through translation, the silencing of women's contributions to society as translators and writers and, more generally, the non-recognition of women as influential actors in culture and writing' (2011, p. 2).

She adds that there have been many editorial and translation projects focussed on women's writing, such as anthologies or scholarly works (2011, p. 2), aiming to make women's writing visible and available. What might be considered key here is the very act of calling attention to a work by a woman, by publishing it at all and particularly by publishing it in translation, perhaps even with scholarly apparatus attached to it, which could emphasise its importance (although arguably a text is not important solely by dint of who wrote it). Translating women's writing, then, is potentially about challenging ideas about who is considered worthy of speaking and being heard in a given society or situation.

Gayatri Chakravorty Spivak writes that the first step is that 'the translator must surrender to the text' and earn 'the right to become the intimate reader' (1992/2004, p. 372), and she emphasises the importance of 'agency' when it comes to women's writing, as agency is particularly an issue for women generally in the world, as already noted (1992/2004, p. 373). Carol Maier suggests possible strategies for translating women's fiction, even while acknowledging the slipperiness of the concepts 'woman' and 'women's writing' (1998, p. 99). Her first strategy is

> 'the absence of a deliberately formulated method. The absence of an acknow-ledged approach does not necessarily imply carelessness, however, nor is it purely negative. Many highly successful translators discuss their work by detailing problems and solutions but without defining principles. They often express a refusal to work analytically, affirming instead "spontaneity" or "creativity." For such "null" strategists, "What is woman?" would not be a question, and there would be no definition of "woman." The translator would not feel a need for one' (1998, p. 98).

This absence of strategy perhaps could be better explained as translating a piece of woman's writing as if it is any other sort of text, which, of course, it is, and focussing on certain stylistic aspects rather than its genre or authorship or intended readership.

Maier's second strategy is at what she terms 'the opposite end of the continuum' (1998, p. 99), and this is a feminist strategy. She writes that as with the lack of specific strategy, a feminist strategy feels no need to define the term woman but instead is shaped by a 'simultaneous affirmation and refusal', which means 'affirming women writers through a refusal to translate work written by men, often choosing to translate only explicitly feminist texts' (1998, p. 99). A feminist strategy might not require defining 'woman', but it appears to require a definition for 'feminist'. This is not as paradoxical as it may seem. But a further complication is that some refer to 'feminine' strategies (see later, regarding Massardier-Kenney 1997). Woman, feminist and feminine are, obviously, not the same.

Maier then suggests a third method, which is somewhere between the two aforementioned strategies and involves some sort of attention to defining 'woman'. She writes that '[i]t is possible to think of these degrees primarily with respect to a translator's identification or definition of her, or his, own work – in other words to associate them with translators who either identify themselves as women or work with authors identified as women' (1998, p. 100).

However, Maier herself finds this problematic, for reasons she explores in her article. Maier writes,

'I have come to think of working not as a woman-identified translator, but as one who questions, even interrogates gender definitions – one who can hold "natural" definitions of gender in abeyance, attempting to identify one's practice as a translator in a way that is open to and can thus interact with whatever gender identity (or other identity) a translator might encounter. It would be appropriate to think of this approach as "woman-interrogated" ... ' (1998, p. 102).

This seems to suggest that anyone, of any gender identity, could translate work by authors who identify or are identified as women, and that they could do so in a gender-interrogative way if they so choose; although beyond the scope of this Element, it is worth pointing out that given current debates about identity politics and translation – such as the recent furore about whether the work of a young Black female poet could be translated by someone who was not Black (e.g. Holligan 2021) – I am not sure everyone today would agree with Maier's standpoint. On the other hand, the Warwick Prize for Women in Translation goes to a work 'written by a woman, translated into English by a translator (or translators) of any gender' (Warwick Prize website 2021), which suggests that for some, like Maier, the question of the author's gender matters more than the translator's. Whose gender matters, or matters more?

Maier closes by stating that 'translating women's fiction emerges as a translator's rewriting of fiction written by a woman, as "woman" is defined by the translator with respect to a particular instance of translation' (1998, p. 108). Here, then, translating women's writing differs according to the individual translator's own definition of 'woman' and perhaps their own gender identity, and also by the level of woman-interrogative methodology or strategising they employ.

But some go even further than this. While Maier only briefly mentions feminist translation methods, Von Flotow, along with others such as Susanne de Lotbinière-Harwood and Sherry Simon, both also from the Canadian school, have developed and champion a variety of approaches under this heading. As already suggested, the term 'woman' is not the same as the term 'feminist' and neither is it the same as 'feminine'; that is, whatever women might or might not be, not all women are feminists, not all women's writing is feminist writing, not all female translators want to employ feminist strategies, not all women or feminists are feminine, not all feminist strategies would be the same as feminine ones and so on. Still, some translators find it important to choose strategies that emphasise the gender of the author and/or characters; this could be said to be gender-interrogative, as Maier terms it, but with a slightly different angle.

The strategies, some of which were mentioned earlier in regard to historical feminist approaches, tend to centre on highlighting gender or gender stereotypes and can also include adding in or deleting references to gender. Von Flotow and Simon have recommended a number of different feminist translation tactics, including supplementing, prefacing and footnoting and hijacking (Simon 1996, p. 14, and see von Flotow 1991 and 1997 as well). Meanwhile, de Lotbinière-Harwood recommends the employment of notes or even more radical changes, such as invented spellings (Conacher 2006, p. 250). Kim Wallmach, borrowing from the work of other scholars, such as Dirk Delabastita, categorises feminist translation strategies as 'substitution, repetition, deletion, addition and permutation' (2006, p. 15), and then offers further sub-methods, such as 'compensation by footnoting' and 'compensation by splitting' (2006, p. 18); she notes that these are all methods that can be used across translation and not just in feminist translation, but that there are specifically feminist ways of employing them.

Castro and Ergun offer additional strategies that have been developed by scholars and translators beyond Canada. Examples include Suzanne Jill Levine's work 'subverting' misogynistic texts, sometimes with the original author's permission (2018, p. 129), or Carol Maier adding female characters (2018, p. 129), or other translators using gender-inclusive language, such as when translating religious texts (2018, p. 130). Elizabeth Ann Remington Willett suggests that the use of punctuation and formatting can be feminist strategies as well (2016, p. 402). In China specifically, Zhongli Yu mentions how 'rewriting, domesticating, and addition' are possible approaches for the 'transmission of Western feminism in China' (2017, p. 61), but it is worth mentioning that it may be more desirable at times to adapt women's writing to Chinese feminism and/or to bring Chinese feminist perspectives across to the West. Along those lines, Sun Kyoung Yoon explores translation from Korean to English and argues that what some critics perceive to be 'mistranslations' are actually feminist interventions that reveal and question patriarchal aspects of Korean society (2020, p. 939). Such methods can take place in retranslations as well. A new translation of the Arabian Nights – the first one by a woman, Yasmine Seale – works as a 'riposte' to earlier translations, adding back in stories about women that had previously been omitted and 'stripping away the Orientalism and the added, interpolated racism and sexism' (Flood, 2021b, n. p.). Such a translation is said to 'break' with previous ones and to allow for new, perhaps fuller interpretations of the text.

Castro and Ergun make the important point that most of the strategies discussed in scholarly literature focus on literary texts, but of course are also applicable to non-fiction works, such as advertisements or legal documents, especially as more non-fiction is translated than fiction (2018, p. 130). While here I am primarily referring to fiction, I think it is essential to acknowledge that translators can and do make interventions in other types of writing too.

Von Flotow suggests that 'socially-activist and implicitly feminist approaches that examine identity, power and visibility continue to bear fruit' (2011, p. 9) but not everyone would agree with this statement or with the sorts of strategies discussed here. For example, Wallmach discusses the idea that some people have that 'a feminist translation becomes a deliberate mistranslation and extension of the source text, and that feminist translation practice, unlike conventional translation practice, constitutes difference and not derivation' (2006, p. 2). While some might see this 'deliberate mistranslation and exten-sion' as positive, others feel that the translator is overstepping the bounds of their role. Some argue that a translator needs to translate just what is on the page, not allowing their own opinions or experiences to colour how they translate. But can a translator ever completely ignore their own identity, as Maier seems to insist upon?

Another criticism is that '[i]f we look at the explanation of these [feminist] strategies, we find that it is not the strategies themselves that are *feminist*, assuming the notion of *feminist* itself is clear and non-controversial, but rather the use to which these strategies are put' (Massardier-Kenney 1997, p. 57, emphasis in original). To make it clearer, Françoise Massardier-Kenney notes that '[w]hat is feminist then is the use to which this strategy is put in order to emphasize the woman's point of view that was present in the source text and that the translator is determined to carry over' (1997, p. 57). Massardier-Kenney critiques what she terms the idea of making the 'feminine' visible and writes that

> 'feminist translators should be aware that they are adapting existing transla-tion strategies rather than inventing new ones. The major strategies that have been or can be adapted to advance a feminist agenda (i.e. to problematize the minimization of what is defined as the feminine or as woman/women) can be fruitfully categorized as author-centred or translator-centred. Author-centred strategies include recovery, commentary and resistancy; translator-centred strategies include commentary, use of parallel texts and collaboration'
>
> (1997, p. 58).

She defines recovery as 'consist[ing] of the widening and reshaping of canon' (1997, p. 59); commentary as 'metadiscourse accompanying the translation to make explicit the importance of the feminine or of woman/women (either in terms of structural constraints or in terms of women's agency) in the text translated' (1997, p. 60) and resistancy as 'making the labour of translation visible through linguistic means that have a defamiliarizing effect and that work against easy fluency' (1997, p. 60). In terms of translator-centred strategies, commentary here is where a 'feminist translator must describe her motives and the way they affect the translated text in order to avoid reproducing a textual power structure which genders the translator as the male confessor of the text' (1997, p. 63); the use of parallel texts means 'texts in the target language that were produced in a similar situation or that belong to the same genre as that of the source text' (1997, p. 64), although this implies that she does not necessarily view women's writing as a genre; and collaboration means working with the author and/or other translators (1997, p. 64–5). Some of these ideas seem similar to what others have previously recommended, and I would suggest that the term 'feminine' is as problematic as woman or feminist. Massardier-Kenney concludes by stating that the use of such strategies

> 'leads us to reconsider the object of translation not as a text to serve or to master, but as a cultural event to *re-present*. The feminist recognition that this *re-presentation* involves an elusive notion of the feminine means that we need to examine the various ways in which gender is connected to or disconnected from the text, and the way it relates to the specific mode of representation claimed by feminist translators' (1997, p. 65, emphasis in original).

Spivak, although focussed in particular on what she terms 'Third World' writing by women, argues that translating work by women is a political act, one related to showing solidarity, and that a translator must make the 'translated text accessible . . . for the person who wrote it', because '[t]he accessible level is the level of abstraction where the individual is already former, where one can speak individual rights' (1992/2004, p. 379). In other words, it is political – not necessarily feminist, although often so – to learn other languages (1992/2004, p. 379) and to make texts from those languages available in other tongues.

I think that regardless of what term one uses – feminist translation, feminine translation, political translation, translation out of solidarity, gender-interrogative strategies, the translation of women's writing and so on – it appears that there is some agreement that an approach or, at the very least, thoughtfulness is needed when it comes to works that are in some way by and about women and women's issues, ideally something that reveals or comments on power, gender and society. Wallmach finds that 'feminist translation pro-vides an admirable demonstration of the workings of ideology in texts. It illustrates how a principle, or a belief, linked to power relationships (in this case, the power of the word written by woman) is transmuted, through language, as an effect of discourse, and becomes naturalised. What is a belief or an attitude which could be challenged or contradicted is constructed by language and through language as a reality, as an incontrovertible fact of the feminist world' (2006, p. 23). The overall idea often seems to be that writing by and about women requires more attention to gender, emotions, experiences, identity, politics and so on than writing by and about men (there is not yet enough trans or non-binary literature to state anything firmly about where it might fit in here). A possible question is whether translators of texts by and/or about women need to be women themselves, or whether male or non-binary translators may be considered able to translate these texts, if they employ women-centred or feminist approaches. And, as already noted, intersectional approaches are needed and have only recently been developing; 'by inviting intersectional approaches to translation, [we can] challenge and complicate earlier approaches to feminist translation that almost exclusively focused on gender, framed habitually in Western-centric, binary and essentialist terms' (Castro and Ergun, 2018, p. 135).

So perhaps we can summarise this section by stating that some, if not all, work by and about women and women's lives requires particular attention and effort in translation. For many, highlighting the work of women is an important political act, rectifying years and generations of women and their writing being ignored and erased. There are a variety of ideas about how to go about this, but for many, attending to issues of gender is a key aspect of the work a translator of women's writing must do.

Genre 2: Drama

Definitions

One dictionary definition of drama is 'a play in a theatre or on television or radio, or plays and acting generally' (Cambridge 2021, n.p.); although the use of the term 'play' suggests that written works are covered by this definition, the overarching sense of the word here emphasises the performative nature of drama, regardless of where or in what medium. Marvin Carlson notes that humans are storytelling creatures – perhaps it is this that differentiates us from other animals – and that drama or theatre could be understood as 'embodied practice' (2014, p. 1). Carlson offers a loose definition of drama as 'A impersonates B while C looks on' (2014, p. 2), where A is the one performing, B is the human, animal, plant, inanimate object or whatever else A is imitating and C is the audience. In other words, there is an expectation of an audience, generally one that watches while the actors are performing or else watches a recording of a performance (cf. Edgar 2009, pp. 1–13); there is an awareness 'that what we [the audience] are seeing is mediated and intentional' (Edgar 2009, p. 13). Of course printed works, whether plays or otherwise, have an audience, too, but it is usually one that reads the work silently (except in the case of children's literature, as discussed later in this text). However, plays are often, though not always, written down before being performed, and it is this written form that a translator works with, which suggests that a translator must be aware of performativity and yet is not part of the visible performance. This will be returned to below.

Drama is a very broad category. David Edgar writes that '[h]istorically, the stage has been dominated by theatre, opera and ballet' (2009, p. 64). Within the theatre category, Carlson refers to storytelling, puppetry, theatre, opera, melodrama and history as general types (2014, pp. 1–17), and then further specifies 'domestic middle-class drama' (2014, p. 23), symbolism, expressionism, epic theatre, absurd, indigenous theatre styles (2014, p. 23), immersive theatre and readymades (2014, p. 25), commedia dell'arte (2014, p. 54), performance art and happenings (2014, p. 75), among others. There is tragedy, kabuki, pantomime, comedy, political theatre, experimental theatre, farce, one-person show, musical theatre and more types. I also wonder whether, for example, burlesque, stand-up comedy, storytelling, dinner theatre, performance/slam poetry, installations, mime, revue, vaudeville, skits, lieder and so forth might be considered to be part of this field of work; Edgar refers to circus and variety as well (2009, p. 64). Some are quite interactive and require involvement and feedback from the audience; for example, performances of *The Rocky Horror Picture Show* may involve both the film playing and also people from the audience getting on stage in costume, acting out parts of the show. Not all people would consider this a form of drama, but some would. Furthermore, there is a range of styles and subjects within these categories listed here and all this varies from one culture to another (e.g. Zatlin 2006, p. 3, where she discusses how each language/culture has its own stylistics and conventions), which, as with the other genres discussed in this Element, means that theatre or drama is a very large genre containing multiple genres too, creating further distinctions.

So then the question becomes how to distinguish drama from another text type. Edgar writes that '[m]uch more useful for playwrights is the idea of genre as a set of expectations of storyline, character, locale and outcome. Any discussion of genre exposes theatre's dirty little secret, which is that audiences know the ending of most plays (or certainly the *sort* of ending) before they begin' (2009, p. 65, emphasis in original). This returns to the importance of the audience. We must distinguish between plays on the page and plays on the stage; along these lines, Sirkku Aaltonen distinguishes between 'theatre translation' and 'drama translation' (2000, p. 4), and to go one step further, there are also plays on the page for general consumption and those intended as scholarly editions, with essays and/or footnotes and/or other information to increase reader comprehension.

In terms of the page, plays may look different from other genres. To be very specific about the conventions one finds in a playscript, which may separate it from other text types, I could mention items such as acts and scenes, naming all the characters in a list before the play proper, noting when someone enters or exits, and also primarily including monologues, dialogues and conversations versus prose descriptions of, for instance, characters' appearances or backstory, unless such descriptions were offered by a narrator or character. Naturally, not all playwrights follow these conventions.

Though Edward W. Rosenheim, Jr's work is dated, it is still applicable in its basic understanding of drama; in short, he discusses how the print version of a play is different from a performance for the audience (1961, p. 96). To name a few differences, when reading, the audience imagines the setting and what the characters look and sound like, but when viewing the performance, such details are shown and audience members are thus less active in their interaction with the work. When reading a play, there might be some extratextual descriptions of characters or the setting or stage directions regarding the tone of voice or a movement someone makes, but the reader must guess and imagine quite a lot; this could be considered quite demanding. But a viewer of a performance, while not exactly only a passive consumer, is given much more information; the actors and director will have made choices, some of which may accord with what the playwright has written or what the reader would have imagined, but others of which may challenge authorial intentions or viewer expectations or go beyond what the printed word suggests. The audience members see how people move and gesture, hear their voices, consider the props, see what the set is like, have their attention focussed by lighting, understand the characters better by their looks or clothing choices or hairstyle or make-up and so forth. There are many stimuli, which means more for the viewer to consider and make sense of, along with the actual words.

In other words, while reading is generally a solitary experience in which the reader is the chief interpreter of the work, when in the audience at a theatre, much of the interpretation has been carried out already. The director, actors, stage designers, lighting directors, costume designers, producers and others will all have added their ideas and readings, and the viewer then must base their understanding and opinions on that multi-layered interpretation. Rosenheim feels that audience expectations are such that audiences know what it means to go to the theatre; they recognise that reality is an 'illusion' (1961, p. 106) and they are thus prepared to make 'concessions' (1961, p. 117), and I would suggest that part of this means giving up some control over interpretation, which may be to a certain extent what some people enjoy. In translation, the translator may well have added layers of interpretation, based on their own understanding or their ideas about what the audience might need or expect.

Besides the very fact of performability, the experience of reading versus viewing drama differs because when reading, a reader can flip back to a previous page and re-read it, or skip ahead, while they are forced to move forward in time at a pace decided upon by the actors when in the audience at a theatre (watching it on TV or film may allow for back-and-forth movement, however). Not being able to turn back to an earlier page requires the audience to remember what they have seen and to possess the ability to make connections during a relatively short period of time. Rosenheim notes that 'drama is not ordinarily created to be studied by reflective persons at convenient moments' (1961, p. 106). A performance is 'intrinsically ephemeral' and '[s]itting in the house, the audience has just one chance to register what's going on: no pages to flip, no rewind, no instant replay. And that beautiful phrase you so toiled to achieve can vanish in a cough or be cut by one missed cue' (Boehm, 2001, p. 28). This can, of course, have both positive and negative implications.

Drama, then, is a large generic grouping that covers many types of work, both on the page and/or on the stage. It can be about anything and it can be written and performed in many different styles. That is to say that to analyse and then translate a dramatic work means to first try to understand the conventions around the particular subtype and the culture it is situated in it while understanding that the translator will be one of many other interpreters involved in the creation of a piece for performance.

Translation

Andrea Peghinelli writes,

> 'Theatre translation is usually seen as a more complex dimension of literary translation since the text being translated is thought to be just one of the elements of theatre discourse that one has to render in a different language. Besides, theatre is a mirror of the world, a mirror that not only reflects the verbal utterances but also actions, gestures, silences and the whole apparatus that goes together with them. That is why in translating for theatre the intrinsic impossibility of translation becomes an even more complicated process' (2012, p. 21).

And yet, this complicated process must be attempted, and often an attempt must start with what is on the page, before the translator can consider what happens on the stage.

Geraldine Brodie points out that there are two types of translator potentially involved in theatre translation: the indirect translator and the direct translator

(2017, pp. 128–34). The latter carries out an actual translation, while the former – sometimes also called the 'surrogate translator' – turns that version into something that is performed. The indirect translator might not know the source language and/or might be a playwright or director or someone with a well-known name that could draw in crowds to see the play. The direct translator, in such a situation, may not get much credit. (This can happen in other fields too, notably poetry and children's literature.)

Meanwhile, Joseph Che Suh offers a range of terms for what translators might do when working on drama; there is translation, but he also refers to adaptation, rewriting, versioning and transplanting, noting how such terms are not always clearly defined and may vary from scholar to scholar (2002, p. 53). This perhaps implies that translating drama requires different strategies and approaches than translating other forms of work; indeed, Suh writes that translating drama is not about 'mere textual transfer' but rather 'cultural mediation and interchange' (2002, p. 52). Phyllis Zatlin seems to also suggest that translators of drama must adapt or change more than other types of translators (2006, p. 3), and notes that transplanting may require wholesale rewriting (2006, p. 72) and could change the work significantly (2006, p. 79). But, as she notes, it may be the only strategy possible (2006, p. 81). So someone who is working on transforming a dramatic work from one language and culture to another would have to consider which of these tasks they are carrying out and why (and, potentially, as Brodie notes, who else is involved in the translation).

Besides that, or related to that, is whether to translate (or adapt, rewrite, etc.) for the page or the stage, or whether it is possible to do both (e.g. Zatlin 2006, p. 67 on acting versus reading). Ideally, the client – the publisher, for example, or the director/theatre – would tell the translator whether the translation was going to be printed or performed or both, and this might impact particular choices a translator makes. Che Suh talks about the importance of the 'initiator' or commissioner in this regard; the director or theatre or dramaturge or whoever wants this work translated will have opinions about how it is transferred and will 'inevitably or invariably compel the drama translator to adopt' particular strategies (2002, p. 56). Equally, it may not be known what the ultimate function of the translation is to be. So before even starting to look at the content, the *skopos* needs to be understood; this relates back to the recurring discussion of audience expectations in this Element.

Along with such choices, a translator may need to do research. In an analysis of the literal translations of a particular translator whose work is considered in the branch to be 'best practice', Brodie highlights how this translator, Helen Rappaport, takes a 'scholarly approach' (2018, p. 214). This approach means researching a play's performances and publications, the cultural allusions in the work, the cultural context, and much more, and writing notes and annotations on all these angles and nuances (2018, p. 215). This information can be of benefit to the actors and directors and also to any additional playwrights, scholars or others who use Rappaport's translations as the basis for their own version of the original play (see Brodie 2017, pp. 128–33 for more on this). Zatlin certainly agrees that translators need to do research in order to understand the historical context (2006, p. 73); while this is a useful suggestion, not all translators have the time or the access to the necessary resources to do this. Research or work with a translator with the same language pairing, but perhaps in the opposite direction, may be necessary for dealing with specific literary or cultural allusions or with idioms; as Zatlin ruefully notes, a person reading a work while alone may overlook a mistake but an audience together may react quite differently to a 'howler' (2006, p. 86).

Jozefina Komporaly, herself a translator of drama, seems to agree with the idea of research when she discusses how a translator must analyse and be aware of 'the playwright's political and aesthetic concerns' and also consider any 'political responsibility' involved in translation, depending on the languages and cultures being translated from and to (2021, p. 167). And yet, despite the potential need for this sort of work, Che Suh notes that there traditionally has been a linguistic focus when it comes to the translation of drama, presumably because plays are usually meant to be spoken aloud and performed (2002, p. 52); close attention to the translation of words does make sense, but there are multiple types of word in a play, not just those spoken. As was discussed earlier, drama contains many conventions in both writing and performance, so translators 'need to familiarize themselves with terminology and style for stage directions in the target language' (Zatlin 2006, p. 67). As Zatlin points out, there is no use translating stage directions literally because conventions can vary; one example is how stage left and right in some cultures is described from the perspective of the actor, while in other cultures, it is from the view of the audience (2006, p. 68).

Komporaly writes about the types of approaches she takes in her work, and this offers ideas for other translators. For example, her first method for one play was 'a relatively open text, in fairly neutral language, that felt like a blank slate that could be explored in rehearsal' (2021, p. 169). She then attempted 'a literal version', trying to stay close to the playwright's choices in regard to register in particular (2021, p. 169). After having actors perform this version, Komporaly found that she had to make additional interventions in the text, so that it would work better in translation, even if it was different from the original (2021, p. 170). Following this, she 'smuggled', as she phrases it, words from the source language into the target text, to try to retain some of the 'otherness' of the original (2021, p. 171). In sum, Komporaly calls this a 'process of collective creation with the performers over an extended period of time' (2021, p. 171) because she was able to produce different drafts and get feedback from the performers, and this in turn enabled further refinement. Peghinelli, too, emphasises the collaborative nature of drama translation and considers the translator a co-creator on a par with the playwright, the dramaturge and director (2012, p. 23), while Philip Boehm calls this collective process 'reshaping' and refers to the 'shifting' nature of drama translation (2001, p. 27). Komporaly adds, 'translations need to be developed with the help and for the benefit of their originals, in full knowledge of the source and receiving cultures and the particular agendas of the creative teams' (2021, p. 173).

Sirku Aaltonen has a different list of methods, describing three categories for the methods of translating plays, with various approaches within the methods. She writes, 'texts may be translated in their entirety; or only partially with various types of alteration; or they may be based on some idea or theme from the source text' (2000, p. 8). She goes on to describe possible attitudes towards translation: '[r]everence characterises the choice of both the text and translation strategy when the "foreign" represents desirable cultural goods' while, on the other hand, there is subversion, '[w]hen the foreign source texts are seen primarily as material for the indigenous stage or expressive of domestic issues, they are subverted to serve the needs of the target system and society through strategies which rewrite them to fall in line with the discourse of the target society' (2000, p. 8). Aaltonen also reminds us that, 'The dramatic text is only one of the elements of a *mise en scène*, and there are other equally important elements in it which can guarantee either its success or its failure if allowed to do so' (2000, p. 37, italics original). Still, clearly, how the text is translated does matter.

Zatlin discusses strategies in light of ideas about domestication and foreignization – how much a translator should move the text to the audience and adapt it to their culture, language and understanding versus how much of the original to retain (e.g. Venuti 1995; foreignization could be viewed as the ethical choice because it forces the reader to the work and to move towards the text). Zatlin also adds an approach that is not quite either of those two: the concept of translating/adapting a text so it better conforms to audience expectations of the source culture or people (2006, p. 69). Another strategy she mentions is downplaying the source location or culture (2006, p. 70); this sounds like domestication, but is not quite the same in that, for example, Beijing is not transformed into London but rather the Chineseness, if one can put it that way, of Beijing is 'under-translated' or generalised, as Zatlin puts it (2006, p. 70).

Besides the choice of direct or indirect translator, the choice to translate the whole play or only part of it, the choice to translate for the stage or the page, and the choice to translate with 'reverence' or 'subversion', as Aaltonen suggests, there are more choices to be made when it comes to strategies. The range of approaches already mentioned – domestication, foreignization, emphasising and downplaying/generalising – reveals that Che Suh is correct when he writes that there is 'no consensus' when it comes to strategies for translation drama (2002, p. 54); Zatlin, too, writes there is 'no single correct answer' (2006, p. 73). For example, she argues against extratextual material, finding it to be a 'not viable solution' (2006, p. 71). On the other hand, audience members at theatres may get playbills and some may enjoy reading additional information about the work, despite Zatlin's concerns. However, Zatlin seems to go for intertextual glosses and occasional over-translation, as a way of explaining particular items (2006, p. 72), which is a strategy that other translators – or indeed the audience – may not approve of or enjoy. In terms of names specifically, for instance, she writes that if 'foreign names are unpronounceable or have unwanted connotations in the target language, change is clearly required' (2006, p. 73). Zatlin discusses considering how to have an equivalent impact on the audience (2006, p. 79) as an overriding concern.

There is also a question of whether particular aspects of language in drama or specific forms of drama need different translation strategies (Zatlin, for example, explores subtitling and dubbing, which are potentially relevant types of translation that I will not discuss here for reasons of space constraints (2006, pp. 123–49)). Zatlin writes that there is 'less flexibility' in historical work, because of the need for fidelity in regard to historical facts (2006, p. 73).

In some, perhaps many, cases, the performability aspect does take precedence. Zatlin argues that translating drama is harder than translating poetry, because, although similar in scope, the performative aspect makes it more challenging, in her opinion (2006, p. 75); of course poetry can be performed too, but is usually less dependent on features such as lighting, setting, movement, gestures and the overall performance.

Due to the importance of language, Zatlin claims that slang and dialect in particular may require adaptation (2006, pp. 81–2). She cites Manuela Perteghella, who suggests five strategies for dialect in particular: dialect compilation (using some target dialect but keeping the original setting), pseudo-dialect translation (using a made-up dialect), parallel dialect translation (using a target language dialect with similar associations to the original dialect), dialect localisation (domestication, or using a target setting and dialect) and standardisation (using standard forms of language rather than dialect) (2006, pp. 83–4); similar strategies can be used for slang (2006, p. 85). Also, there is a larger issue in terms of differing forms of a language. To start with, there are dialects, and a play being translated to, for example, Spanish, might need one translator for

Spain, another for Argentina, another for Costa Rica and so on, or at the very least one translator to Spanish and then editors/reviewers who can adapt the Spanish as necessary (e.g. Zatlin 2006, pp. 15–16). Another related issue is how some languages have spoken versus literary languages (e.g. Lathey 2015, p. 73, in regard to the example of Arabic) or versions of languages that are spoken depending on the gender of the person speaking or being spoken to (e.g. Lathey 2015, p. 74). That is, what is acceptable to say orally might not be considered appropriate in the written format and what is appropriate for one set of actors might not be appropriate in another situation, which would suggest the potential need to have one translation for the page and one for the stage, or multiple translations. Of course, one could point out that many of these strategies could be used for other text types, but the emphasis on the need to perform the words perhaps means that translators must think particularly in-depth about language usage in drama.

Che Suh implies that a translator ought to focus on the audience and the reception of the text (2002, p. 55). On the other hand, Zatlin argues that translators need to focus more on the actors who will speak their words (2006, p. 4). This makes some sense as translators have to, as already noted, consider how their work will be performed. This also means considering speakability – whether the words can actually be spoken and whether they work well together – as well as musicality; the latter is perhaps especially relevant to more poetic works or to musical, operas, operettas and so forth, but the rhythm and flow of the words matters in general. But the focus on what the actors will need to say and do implies that translators are more like authors; I would in fact argue that translators are usually co-authors, depending on the text type and functions and strategies, but perhaps when it comes to drama, due to the apparent increased need for adaptation, translators must be particularly active in their choice of approaches. Indeed, Zatlin says that translators might want to be involved in rehearsals, to see how their words work in practice (2006, p. 5) (other scholars comment on this as well, such as Komporaly 2021). She writes that translators need to consider the rhythm of the words and to ensure that they fit with the characters' gestures and movements (2006, p. 74), and also to consider the speed of spoken language in both the source and target languages (2006, p. 75–7).

Finally, Zatlin notes how important the title is to get right in translation because it is key for marketing the play (2006, p. 95). Citing Peter Newmark, she differentiates between descriptive and allusive titles; Newmark suggests translating the former as they are and adapting the latter as and when necessary (2006, p. 95). But Zatlin adds that titles must be translated and not kept in the original language and that it is essential to consider the market, as different countries have different expectations about titles (2006, pp. 96–7); for example, '[t]he American stage leans heavily towards realism/naturalism', which might mean that 'allusive titles that are long and poetic' might not work there (2006, p. 97).

Performativity and performability have been referred to in different ways through this section on drama, and it feels right to close by discussing the translator's role in this. The translator, as already discussed here, must consider the performability of the dramatic work while translating, particularly if translating for the stage, but there is another aspect to performance to consider. Translating itself is a performance; I would argue, although not all translators would agree with me, that the translator must in some way enact the author or character's role in order to fully understand and inhabit the story and to be able to bring it across to the target language. This does not mean that translators of drama must themselves be actors or directors or others intimately familiar with drama, although that could help and some might argue that it is essential. Additionally, the translator needs to consider the audience and to perform for the readers (or viewers, in the case of drama); we have to think about the readers' expectations, needs, perspectives and wishes and then we must meet or subvert them as appropriate. Stage actors receive immediate feedback from their audience, in that they can see if the audience is moved or amused or whatever it might be, and they can adjust their acting to this if necessary, while translators can for the most part only imagine and attempt to predict responses. Robert Weschler writes that the translator's problem is that he [sic] is a performer without a stage' (1998, p. 7). I do not fully agree that this is a problem and even if it is, there are ways around it, such as by reading drafts of translations aloud to people or having them read and comment on work in progress and thereby getting feedback, but it is certainly true that we are usually performers without a stage and that performance and performability imbues our work, whether we are translating drama or any other text type.

Genre 3: LGBTQ+ Literature

Definitions

Understanding LGBTQ+ literature requires that we start by defining the acronym. By LGBTQ+, I am referring to a very broad range of gender identities and sexualities – lesbian, gay, bisexual, trans, queer, kink, intersex, genderqueer, non-binary, non-monogamous, polyamorous, asexual, aromantic, pansexual and more (e.g. Sullivan 2003/2011, pp. 1–19) – and I must acknowledge that people who identify with one or more of those labels may not necessarily want to be grouped with the others. Equally, people may recognise themselves in descriptions of particular identities – for example, a woman attracted to other women – but refuse a label that others may give them – for example, gay or lesbian or queer. 'Queer' is often considered the overarching term, and is certainly used in academia, as in queer theory (see, for example, Sullivan 2003/2011), but it is a word that some recoil from while others embrace it, and it is quite difficult to define because our understanding of gender and sexuality continues to evolve. Here, however, I find it beneficial, as will become clear later in the text, so I will use queer and LGBTQ+ somewhat interchangeably. I acknowledge that it is complicated that we have an umbrella term that may or may not be understood and also may or may not be wanted by those who could technically be under that umbrella. LGBTQ+ people exist in every other category of people – in every class, race, ethnicity, religion, ability and so forth – and are certainly not monolithic, so attempting to put them into one category could result in stereotypes or limitations, but on the other hand, joining together can also create a strong political movement (such as Stonewall).

If we do assume for the moment that LGBTQ+ writing, or perhaps queer writing, could be a genre, what is it? As with the category of women's writing, I immediately question the idea that LGBTQ+ literature is its own genre. And yet, it too is often seen that way, at least in some countries; bookstores and libraries have particular sections for their 'queer selections', such as the 'Loud and Proud' collection here at some of the libraries in Norfolk, England, where I live, and sometimes they even label such books with a rainbow sticker, notwithstanding the fact that perhaps not everyone feels able to be out and proud about their gender or sexuality, or even about what sort of literature they are reading.

Perhaps, as for women's writing, LGBTQ+ literature is work by an LGBTQ+ author. But this is difficult for a number of reasons. To start with, who gives an author that label? Is it the author or the reader? As already noted, not everyone who could be called LGBTQ+ uses that label; they may not want to be visible or known in that way, or they may not feel that the term reflects their true identity, or they may not have the term or concept 'queer' – or its equivalents or its subsidiaries, if we view it as the umbrella word – in their language or culture. Being LGBTQ+ may be considered immoral or unacceptable in a particular culture or country. The author may also have been writing in a time that understood sexuality or gender identity differently, and it could be anachronistic for a modern audience to slap the writer with a label that would have made no sense to them. Even for a modern writer in the West, they may not want their gender identity or sexuality to be linked to their creative work; for example, the writer Will Davis comments, 'I usually recoil from having my writing defined by my sexuality', in part because of eschewing labels and in part because such a label could dent book sales (2007, n.p.). He also notes there is no 'straight' category for writing, so should queer lit be labelled in this way, setting it in opposition to the 'norm'?

If LGBTQ+ writing cannot be definitively labelled as such based on the author's identification, then perhaps the content of the work is what ensures that a text fits in this category. If we attempt to identify the characters in the work as LGBTQ+, we run into the same issues that we did in regard to authorial identification, in that it may not always be easy to tell if someone is LGBTQ+ and even if one does assume that, the character in question may not identify with the label or it may not suit the historical or cultural context that the character lives in or that the story takes place in.

Another possibility would be to call a text LGBTQ+ if it approaches or deals with LGBTQ+ topics; such topics could include queer identity/identities, rights, politics, activism and more. Some theorists link queerness to migration, implying that queer people – and thereby queer texts and characters – may fluctuate, change and immigrate/emigrate/migrate more than others. 'Sexuality is not only not essence, not timeless, it is also not fixed in place; sexuality is on the move' (Patton and Sanchez-Eppler, 2000, p. 2). A queer topic, then, might have to do with movement or diaspora, and can reveal both actual and figurative movement; a queer person may have to take a journey internally to understand themselves, or externally to find a safe place to live or a community to be part of. Movement is inscribed in the very word 'queer' through its etymological origins; it means 'to twist' or 'across' or 'cross', which perhaps explains why the word has also at times connoted perversity or difference or oddness. Eve Kosofsky Sedgwick writes, 'Queer is a continuing moment, movement, motive . . . it is relational, and strange' (1993, p. xii).

But to focus on queer topics as way of defining the field suggests that LGBTQ+ literature must be issue-driven and/or that an author might be expected to write about LGBTQ+ issues, especially if they themselves identify openly as LGBTQ+, and this could unfairly restrict what an author feels able to explore in their work. As discussed earlier in regard to women's literature and emotions, it is limiting and stereotyping to assume that all works in a particular genre or field must follow particular rules for what they are about.

In addition, LGBTQ+ writing might be defined by its style or its tone. Style was mentioned earlier, with Boase-Beier calling it the form or type of expression (2019, p. 4), and to group LGBTQ+ writing together, we would perhaps need to find a distinctly queer style or tone. An example of an LGBTQ+ tone could be camp, which is 'a specific verbal style . . . [associated] with male homosexual characters' (Harvey 1998, p. 295), but not all LGBTQ+ men across all times and cultures would talk in a camp way, and of course there are queer people of other genders who may or may not use camp speech. Another possible style would perhaps relate to the idea of 'strangeness' embedded in the word 'queer', as mentioned earlier in regard to etymology, but a strange, non-norm style is not something all queer writers would want to use, nor is it simple to define. Given the diversity of people and books that could be called LGBTQ+, it is not possible to define one overarching style. One might hope that LGBTQ+ literature would be open and proud about the author and/or character's gender or sexuality and that this tone of pride would run through the work, but this is simply not the case; see, for instance, Epstein (2013) on LGBTQ+ literature for children and young adults, which often seems to include styles (and subjects) that could be described as sad or negative. As with content, presuming a particularly queer style seems problematic.

The term 'queer' is not only viewed as being a label for someone's gender identity or sexuality, however, and this might be useful for us in regard to definitions. Nikki Sullivan, among others, states that queer is not only a sense of self, a being, but also a verb, a doing: 'to queer – to make strange, to frustrate, to counter act, to delegitimise, to camp up – heteronormative knowledges and institutions, and the subjectivities and socialities that are (in)formed by them and that (in)form them' (2003/2011, p. vi). This means that we could potentially label people, characters or texts as queer – using queer as a noun or an adjective – but we could also talk about queer as a verb. For a writer, queering literature, writing queerly or writing queer or LGBTQ+ literature may in fact mean rejecting labels, including generic ones. For example, analyses of Maggie Nelson's queer book *The Argonauts* often discuss whether the work is memoir, theory, autotheory, romance or something else altogether (e.g. Brennan 2016 or Vickery 2020). Katie Collins notes that '[Nelson's] textual citations lead to her interpenetration by others' writing and reduce the coherence of her authorial self' (2019, p. 311), which suggests that this book, which is about people who are identified as LGBTQ+ and create a family in a non-heteronormative way, is queer in its approach to genre because it refuses to adhere to one specific generic style, and this challenges readers who may have certain expectations about the text they have picked up. An LGBTQ+ text could be one that questions, that que(e)ries, that challenges, that contests, that queers.

So a possible definition of the genre of LGBTQ+ literature is that it is writing that is by or about LGBTQ+ people or topics and/or that it challenges ideas about what literature can be or do. This latter part of the definition implies that it is a genre that defies the very idea of a genre, which clearly means that including such work in a genre called LGBTQ+ or queer literature is problematic at the very least.

Translation

Although the foregoing has raised concerns about grouping wide-ranging texts together under the generic label of LGBTQ+ literature, it is also rather evident that genres can be helpful, for publishers, booksellers/librarians and readers. Someone may want to read a pile of books about the queer experience and would appreciate a list of LGBTQ+ books, while another reader may be looking for information about their own identity, or a bookstore manager may choose to set up a display of works for Pride in the summer, or an editor may need to quickly make a decision about whether to consider a manuscript and if it would fit with their list, and in such cases, knowing that a book is by and/or about LGBTQ+ people or has a queer tone or approach would make their task more expedient. Likewise, a translator might find that calling a text queer could help them select their choice of translatorial strategies.

In the foregoing section, I wrote about employing the word 'queer' as a verb. One can queer something as well as, or instead of, being queer. I would extend this to translation and say that we can queer translation or translate queerly, and this can impact how we translate LGBTQ+ literature. Initial approaches to queer translation were based on the feminist strategies discussed earlier. Luise von Flotow noted that

> 'recently, with the advent of queer theories, the focus on women as a fecund part of gender research abated somewhat, giving way to theories that developed around gay activisms and set aside the neat binary categories expressed through the terms "women" and "men." This led to a spate of texts on gay translation using approaches similar to those inspired by the identity politics in feminist work . . . to work exploring the "closeted" facets of translation and their resonance with homosexuality' (2011, p. 3).

I think von Flotow's term 'gay translation' is limited – since LGBTQ+ literature is more than gay – as are her suggestions about what queer translation can be, but this quote is a good start.

With Keith Harvey (1998) as an exception, in general it was only quite recently that scholars and translators have begun to write about translating LGBTQ+ literature (e.g. Epstein 2010, Epstein and Gillett 2017, Bauer 2015). Analysing, queering or queerying the translation of LGBTQ+ literature can mean a whole range of things, from specific strategies to constructing or questioning identities.

Translating LGBTQ+ literature starts with the choice of which texts to translate. As with women's writing, making previously hidden or disregarded authors and subjects more visible is a vital act. This links to Françoise Massardier-Kenney's references to commentary and recovery (1997, p. 58–9), where publishers, editors and translators may choose certain authors or texts over others and perhaps include commentaries, such as introductions or translator's notes, that increase knowledge of LGBTQ+ people, literature and issues. It may even be that a queer-identified translator uses the choice of work as a deliberate attempt to make their own identity or politics known, or to get certain ideas across.

When carrying out the actual translation, there are additional choices that can be made. Again, taking inspiration from feminist translation strategies, a translator can choose to emphasise the queerness of a text or character or author, or indeed can tone down negative portrayals or stereotypes; likewise, a translator can elide or erase queerness and instead emphasise heteronormative and cisnormative identities, behaviours, attitudes or topics. Based on my own research findings, I have suggested two major strategies for translating LGBTQ+ literature, and I have given them the slightly tongue-in-cheek names of 'acqueering' and 'eradicalisation' (Epstein 2017, p. 121). 'Acqueering' means highlighting or acquiring queerness while 'eradicalisation' means removing queer elements and making LGBTQ+ literature less radical than it might otherwise be (while acknowledging that not all LGBTQ+ texts aim to be or have to be radical at all). Using different terminology, Shalmalee Palekar calls the translation of queer literature either 'interventionist' or 'repressive' (2017, p. 12), which are similar in meaning to my own terms, while William M. Burton employs the term 'inversion' and defines it as 'a turning of the text against itself: inverting the hidden power relations of heterosexism by revealing and underscoring them through techniques borrowed from feminists' (2010, p. 57). Inversion may be more activist or interventionist. In my case studies (2017 and the ongoing research 'Queer Classics in Translation'), I have found that eradicalisation, or repression, is most common as the strategy for LGBTQ+ literature, which perhaps suggests a certain level of discomfort with LGBTQ+ topics and works. Elizabeth Sara Lewis found likewise in her study of subtitles in queer films, writing that 'queer elements in texts, particularly those involving polysemic ambiguity are sometimes not only removed or allowed to be lost in translation, but turned into heteronormative ones' (2010, p. 19).

Acqueering and eradicalisation are broad descriptions of strategies, but it is possible to be even more detailed about approaches to translating LGBTQ+ literature. For example, Emily Rose 'integrates the feminine and masculine symbols [i.e. the Mars and Venus symbols] inside words' (2017, p. 39) when translating trans literature, to emphasise certain aspects of gender. She also at times 'incorporate[s] words which carry gender in English into words which do not' (2017, p. 39); for instance, 'lonesome' becomes 'loneSONe' (2017, p. 40), which forces the reader to consider the male gender. Rose notes that this latter strategy is 'more estranging than the first' (2017, p. 40) while both are attempts to make gender more visible, especially when translating from a gendered language, such as French, to a less-gendered language, such as English. Another strategy Rose has tried is one that 'erase[s] any link to a binary ... [by using] epicene pronouns which would be recognizable to those who take an interest in non-gendered pronouns' (2017, p. 44). Examples might include the use of 'hir' or 'ze', or even 'one'; Rose notes that it can be 'disruptive', but that is the point (2017, p. 44). In her work, Rose also refers to other translators' strategies, such as marking words with 'm' or 'f' in superscript to denote masculine or feminine gender in the source text (2017, p. 42), while Brian James Baer finds a translator who does the opposite and who removes gendered language (2017, p. 58) to make a text that can be read in a differently gendered way than the original was believed to have been intended. Baer also notes that titles can be changed to make the gender of the subject more open to interpretation (2017, p. 59). Rose (2017) believes that some publishers would be eager to publish work translated with such experimental strategies and while this is certainly true, especially because some queer literature aims to test and defy and to force readers to work and think and there is a real place for this in society, not all editors or publishers would be comfortable with it, so such stylistic choices may be more likely to be employed in scholarly works rather than texts for mainstream consumption.

There is also the issue of how to translate queerness itself as an identity. Since the understanding of gender or sexuality is in part culturally and linguistically shaped, an author and their translator may have very different words or concepts at their disposal. Likewise, views of LGBTQ+ topics and people will vary and this too will impact translation. It may require the absorption of words from the source language – such as 'queer' itself – or the creation of new words in the target language, or intertextual or extratextual explanations of identities, terms and behaviours. Shalmalee Palekar writes about how '[q]ueerying translation can also be seen as part of an active *construction* of queer identity across different contexts' (2017, p. 9, emphasis in original). She notes that 'translation is neither an innocent nor a powerless act' (2017, p. 9) and that translators need to be aware of the power they have, perhaps especially when it comes to translating work by or about marginalised groups. Jeffrey Angles finds that translators to Japanese from English focus on LGBTQ+ feelings rather than queerness as an identity (2017, p. 92–3), which has the result of repressing characters' connections to a larger LGBTQ+ community and perhaps implies that same-sex relationships are individual cases rather than being about who a person is in full; this can be considered repressive or eradicalising. Angles suggests that the translation of LGBTQ+ literature can do many things: the works can give the readers 'information about how to behave and how to engage in erotic encounters', or they can offer 'representations of politics and identity' or they can even 'unsettle stereotyped notions about sexuality, including even homo-normative notions of gay identity' (2017, p. 101). This highlights how important LGBTQ+ literature can be; its existence can question, inform and, as Palekar puts it, construct a reader's identity, which is why translators must consider how they translate it and what messages they wish to get across to readers with their translation. This requires very conscious, and conscientious, decision-making.

A question here is whether a translator of a queer text needs to be queer themselves. I raised the topic of identity politics and translation earlier on and do not have a definitive answer, nor could I, but I would suggest that an attentive and sympathetic translator who is willing to carry out research and to expend effort on analysing a text and considering the best approach to translating it is an ideal translator, regardless of their gender or sexuality or any other aspect of their identity. I am well aware that not everyone agrees with me. But no matter a translator's affinity with LGBTQ+ topics and labels, they would do well to remember that there are no neutral translations, as translators are always readers with their own identities and backgrounds and opinions first, who then apply their own interpretations to the text as they translate. So when translating LGBTQ+ literature, translators must make a decision about where they stand on the continuum between acqueering and eradicalisation, or repressing and expressing, the queerness of a text.

Genre 4: Crime Fiction

Definitions

I have called this section crime fiction, but it could equally perhaps be called detective fiction or thrillers or suspense. In other words, before we have even begun to define the genre, it is clear that there are many types or subgenres within it as well as other terms for it. Still, I think crime is a useful overarching title because, in such works, there is nearly always some sort of crime committed, whether it is physical or psychological or both.

Richard Bradford writes that crime has been a subject in literature for at least two millennia (2015, p. 1). Dennis Porter notes,

'Those taking the long view claim that the detective is as old as Oedipus and serendipity or at least eighteenth-century China. Those maintaining the short view assume that detective fiction did not appear before the nineteenth century and the creation of the new police in Paris and London, that its inventor, in the 1840s, was Edgar Allan Poe, and that it reached its golden age in the opening decades of the twentieth century with the nonviolent problem novel' (1981, p. 11).

Porter goes on to discuss the importance of Poe and how his work became in many ways the 'prototype' (1981, p. 27) for detective fiction. Bradford also acknowledges Poe's importance, but recognises Daniel Defoe and Henry Fielding in the century before Poe for their writing about criminality (2015, p. 3), which admittedly is not the same as crime exactly. Still, people have been focussing their plots around crimes for a long time, although it was not until the early eighteenth century that literature, particularly genre fiction, became profitable in English (Bradford 2015, p. 5). The history of crime in literature is long.

Scholars differentiate between different types of crime fiction, and the types of crime fiction that are most written or read at a particular time appear to relate to larger historical and sociocultural factors. For example, Bradford notes that in the British Golden Age of crime fiction, in the 1920s and 1930s and up through about 1954, the 'country-house' or 'gentleman' style of thriller was popular; in such works, the characters were primarily middle class or upper class and there was no 'realism or plausibility' while the story had a 'plot-puzzle formula' (2015, pp. 19–20); he argues that this style of crime fiction was popular for escapist reasons (2015, p. 26). Meanwhile, the American Golden Age, which was around the same period, was entirely different, featuring 'deceit, greed, and sexual potency intercut by a narrative style that is cynical and ruthlessly sardonic' (2015, p. 29). Bradford says the works written and published in the United States were more realistic and he describes them as follows: 'All of the factors that make up realist fiction – characterization, reported speech, situational and spatial context, etc. – are expediencies, subordinate to the intransigent force of clues and potential solutions' (2015, p. 26). Bradford calls UK crime fiction 'whodunit' and the US equivalent 'whydunit' (2015, p. 30). These are just two examples from two countries in approximately the same time period, and this serves to show how varied the works in the crime category can be; readers in the United States versus the United Kingdom in the 1930s, for instance, would have had quite different expectations of the crime fiction they were reading and if translation had been relevant in this case, then the varying styles and expectations surely would have impacted what the translator understood the functions of a given text to be and how the translator thought it should be translated.

One guide to crime fiction lists types including 'standard private eye', with both hard-boiled and soft-boiled versions; cosy mysteries, which feature 'minimal violence, sex, and social relevance; a solution achieved by intellect or intuition rather than police procedure, with order restored in the end; honorable and well bred characters; and a setting in a closed community'; classic or old-fashioned detective stories, which have 'a mysterious death, a closed circle of suspects who all have motives and reasonable opportunity to commit the crime', and of course a detective; police procedurals, which show the workings of the police; thrillers, which show 'threats to the social order, heroes and villains, and deduction and resolution'; and several other types, including 'female sleuth, GLBT [sic] sleuth, historical mysteries, locked door mysteries' and so on (Appalachian State University 2019, n.p., sic). Bradford offers a definition of thriller as a text that 'is characterized by the exaggeration of acts and character-istics that enable the reader to exchange anything resembling credulity for fantasy and escapism' (2015, p. 103), and he also adds horror as one possible subgenre (2015, p. 110) and legal as another (2015, p. 112). Heather Worthington includes children's crime fiction and feminist crime as additional categories (2010, pp. 97, 108).

A big question here is whether crime fiction is a subgenre of literary fiction or if it is something else altogether. While I do not wish to engage in non-productive debates about supposedly highbrow literature versus those books considered to be lowbrow, I must pause over the fact that few crime novels are considered canonical and the canon is what tends to be taught and enshrined as classics. Bradford claims that *To Kill a Mockingbird* is 'the only crime novel classified unequivocally as a literary classic' (2015, p. 112). While I am not sure all scholars would agree with this, it is the case that many people view thrillers as 'commercial', where commercial is contrasted with literary (e.g. Palmer 1979, p. 69). The purported adherence to a formula, and the concept of 'a brand image' (Palmer 1979, p. 69) for a series or for the author, also adds to the feeling that crime fiction is its own genre, one that is perhaps more popular with readers for these reasons; Palmer even puts down readers of crime fiction by claiming they are 'indifferent for all practical purposes, to whether what you are reading is a good, bad or average thriller' (1979, p. 80), which seems to underestimate both readers and the genre (if it is one). It is important to note that Palmer's work is dated, but I think some of those stereotyped ideas remain with us, and thus they are important, given that crime fiction is the most popular form of literature read in English (Johnson 2020, n.p.; cf. Worthington 2010, p. ix). Interestingly, one writer, Paul Bloom, argues that because adults are more familiar with genre, 'children can get more pleasure from thrillers than adults, because they are less conscious of conventions' (2010, p. 185). Given how popular thrillers are among adults, the idea that children enjoy them more does not seem entirely accurate. Perhaps it is truer to say that people, including adults, can get pleasure from thrillers – or other genres – *because* they are conscious of the conventions. They have certain expectations and have ideas about the function of the text, and when those expectations are met, potentially also in a way that is aesthetically pleasing, they enjoy the reading experience, while also not having those expectations met can potentially lead to a stimulating experience too. Worthington writes, 'Crime fiction is at once deeply conservative in its formulaic conventions and yet potentially radically in its diversity' (2010, p. ix).

Bradford sums up the genre by writing that no matter the subtype, crime fiction is about 'constantly gathering evidence, attempting to make sense of patently unreal creations – by definition, puzzles – and close the gap between what we think we know and what the next page will tell us' (2015, pp. 121–2). Given the many subtypes in this genre, it would be useful to think through what characteristics the texts in this field may contain. Palmer suggests that action is a key aspect and that the language usage emphasises the action. He writes that authors 'dramatize a process' so that '[a]ll actions, however mundane, become part of The Action, however insignificant' (1979, p. 78). Palmer mentions other critics, who consider crime fiction 'too corrupt and decadent' (1979, p. 79), but he argues that a good thriller needs 'a hero and a conspiracy' and needs to 'captur[e] the reader's imagination' (1979, p. 80). He adds that 'what is specific to the thriller – what it is that attracts the thriller reader, whether critical or otherwise – is the view of the world that the thriller proposes' (1979, p. 80).

So generally, crime fiction contains action and a puzzle and tells readers something about their society, about ethics and what – or who – is considered 'good' versus 'evil'. The resolution at the end of a crime work shows the values that a society holds dear. Porter writes that popular literature, such as crime fiction, serves as

> 'a reflector and barometer of the society's ideological norms. The importance of popular works resides in their status as meaning-systems that embody implicit world views. Properly interpreted, therefore, they can provide important clues to the anxieties and frustrations, aspirations and constraints, experienced by the mass audience that accounts for their best-seller status' (1981, p. 1).

Ernest Mandel, too, confirms this view and then goes even further, writing,

> 'The history of the crime story is a social history, for it appears intertwined with the history of bourgeois society itself. If the question is asked why it should be reflected in the history of a specific literary genre, the answer is: because the history of bourgeois society is also that of property and of the negation of property, in other words, crime; because the history of bourgeois society is also the growing, explosive contradiction between individual needs or passions and mechanically imposed patterns of social conformism; because bourgeois society in and of itself breeds crime, originates in crime, and leads to crime perhaps because bourgeois society is, when all is said and done, a criminal society?' (1984, p. 135)

That is, Mandel suggests that the Western society we live in is itself criminal and that we may need crime fiction in order to expose this fact to us; this is certainly a view that some crime authors, such as Swedes Maj Sjöwall and Per Wahlöö, subscribe to (*Nordic Noir* 2010).

Related to ideology and the perspective on society, language is a particular issue when it comes to crime fiction. Thrillers may feature different dialects, slang and especially criminal slang, jargon, police terminology, legal terms and more. It stands to reason that if a crime novel features lawyers, police officers, gang members or another specialised group, then their jargon or terminology will be employed in order to make the story seem more realistic and more firmly situated in that particular milieu. Furthermore, characterisation may take place through the language usage; word choice may reveal someone's class or group membership or education, among other things. For instance, '[e]vil or maleficent protagonists can be marked by a special manner of speaking. The use of variational aspects of language (standard and non-standard varieties, colloquial or formal language use, slang, dialect, etc.) can create a social distance between the characters. In addition, the reader can be able to identify the characters or the narrator through language use' (Cadera and Pintarić 2014, p. 13). This contributes both to specific characterisation and to the overall world view mentioned earlier.

The depiction of the genders is also an interesting characteristic when it comes to crime fiction and is similarly related to ideology. Bradford writes that there were few female authors of crime fiction before the UK Golden Age (2015, p. 82), and this may be why the great majority of the characters were male. Women in crime fiction were spinsters and/or victims, and as women were not perceived as rational in society at large, they therefore could not be detectives, whether in reality or in crime fiction (2015, pp. 83–9). While Bradford notes that now there are more women in literature, including lesbians, he feels that 'a genre that emerged as an essentially male-orientated, white, middle-class form of entertainment proves an unusual means of exposing the in-built prejudices of society' (2015, p. 96). So traditionally, crime might be seen as a male genre, although this is continuing to evolve.

In summary, then, crime fiction is a large and diverse field, where the plot generally involves a puzzle or crime that needs to be solved and where readers get a sense of a particular societal perspective through the story, setting, language, depiction of genders and characterisation.

Translation

If ideology is one of the main features of crime fiction, then it stands to reason that translators – who live in a particular time and place and have their own experiences and own views of politics and culture – will have perspectives that must necessarily influence how they translate. Indeed, Worthington explores various critical approaches to analysing crime fiction – such as cultural materialism or postmodernism – which would enable different readings and perspectives on the works (e.g. 2010, pp. 160–5).

I mentioned gender earlier in regard to how women have traditionally been depicted in crime fiction, and I have found in my own research that ideological views of women have apparently impacted how translators translate. For example, in a small research project I carried out into how characters were depicted in crime fiction in Swedish according to their language usage and whether this was changed in translation to English, I discovered that while modern Swedish thrillers were more positive in their portrayal of women than older texts (which were quite misogynist), both the contemporary texts and older texts were translated in a way that suggested a certain level of discomfort with women's agency (2011, n.p.). In Stieg Larsson's *Millennium* series in the original Swedish, for instance, women cursed just as much as men and this was simply part of their normal speech rather than a way of depicting them negatively, but in the translations to English, women's language usage was smoothed out, as if the translator – or editor – felt uncomfortable with women swearing and felt women should be polite and use only standard language.

As the foregoing section on defining crime fiction explored, particular types of language, including dialect, slang, jargon and medical, police, psychological and legal terminology, appear frequently in thrillers. I will not repeat the same suggested strategies on translating dialect that were suggested in the section on the translation of drama, but will note a few things relevant specifically to crime fiction. Susanne M. Cadera and Anita Pavić Pintarić edited a volume on translating 'the voices of suspense' in thrillers, including how suspense is created and how narrative structures can be translated (2014). In one chapter, Sanja Škifić and Rajko Petković argue that the '[r]epetition [of words] is one of the most prominent devices used for creating suspense in different types of narratives' (2014, p. 53). Another specific usage of language that appears often in suspenseful works such as crime fiction (or crime films, which is Škifić and Petković's focus) is swear words (2014, p. 54), and yet another is the '[l]ack of correlation between the content of dialogues and different contexts of the two plots and/or individual characters' (2014, p. 57). Out of these, they note that 'repetition seems to be the most productive linguistic means for creating suspense' (2014, p. 59). Given that words have different connotations in different contexts and also that repetition is often not recommended in writing (e.g. Strunk and White 1935/2000, p. 35), a translator would have to consider which meaning or meanings of the word or phrase to prioritise and whether it should be varied or repeated as it is. Karen Seago also notes that the 'challenge for the translator consists [in some cases] not so much in complex ambiguity but rather in maintaining a stretch of text containing substantial redundancy and not falling into the trap of producing a more cohesive and coherence passage' (2014, p. 216). She writes that repetition is a 'strategy for misdirection which builds on the processing capacity of the reader and it can be used to confuse or to aid recall' (2014, p. 217), and yet she finds that translators tend to remove repetition. The obvious solution, then, would be to retain any repetition instead of varying the language.

Leah Leone explores how suspense, created in part by language and in part by style, can be reconstructed in translation and finds a number of strategies employed by both publishers and translators. In her case study, she finds that a text was apparently censored, which had the effect of 'push[ing]' the female character 'back in line with the heteronormative standards' instead of being allowed to challenge the concept of the femme fatale (2014, p. 83); this is the same as what I found regarding women's language usage in crime fiction. Furthermore, Leone discovers that the translator – Jorge Luis Borges no less – used 'recreation', or rewrote the text in a way that better suited his opinions of what a crime fiction should be; he 'picked up the pace and increased elements of danger and suspense through the elimination of [particular stylistic elements that he did not like]' (2014, p. 84). Leone goes on to give specific examples of how he increased the suspense and changed the relationship between the male and female protagonists in order to adjust them to the 'stable' way he believed gender relations should be; this includes changing line breaks, making sentences more ambiguous so it is unclear who is saying them, and otherwise employing 'inversions and inventions' in order to revise the text, to make it more popular with readers who would have particular expectations of crime fiction and to emphasise particular views of the genders (2014, pp. 84–8). While a translator who is not as famous as Borges may feel unable to make such drastic changes, some of these strategies are certainly available and may be employed, consciously or not, to increase or decrease suspense or to offer a particular view of certain types of people. Leone concludes that '[t]he oft-lamented invisibility of the translator is the perfect cloak behind which one may hide the creative introduction of his or her own literary aspirations into any translation' (2014, p. 89).

Other strategies discussed, which does not mean that they are necessarily recommended, for translating non-standard language in crime fiction include employing an expert on slang in the target language to serve as an advisor for choosing words (Linder 2014, p. 101); adding in a glossary to explain words (Linder 2014, p. 101); compensating by using 'substandard' language (Linder 2014, p. 102); overcompensating to the point of making the text cryptic and needing the addition of a prologue to explain the terms used (Linder 2014, pp. 103–6); using words from a specific dialect in the target language, which may create different connotations for the target readership (Sánchez 2014, p. 122); focussing on cultural or educational register rather than regional dialect (Sánchez 2014, p. 122); normalising or standardising language (Sánchez 2014, p. 123); shifting the oral devices employed due to 'the flexibility of the written language, genre conventions and genre reputation in the different target cultures' (Sánchez 2014, p. 173); and footnotes, although this choice is described as 'less fortunate' because they 'explain culture-specific "untranslatable" elements in an encyclopaedic style [that is] hardly beneficial to maintaining it' (Naro and Naro 2014, p. 190). In short, there are a range of ways of retaining the suspenseful aspects of a crime work, some more useful or successful than others, but all possible tools to consider employing.

Summing up the importance of stylistic features in crime fiction, such as repetition and ambiguity, Seago notes how tricky translating them can be:

> 'Different linguistic structures and cultural contexts do not always permit the translator to maintain instances of ambiguity, allow for the same range of inferences, obscure identification of characters and events or to provide similarly misleading information as in the source text. As a result, most translators of crime fiction will inevitably have instances of over- or under-translation which remove some of the carefully constructed misdirection and rhetorical manipulations in the source text, and produce a text which is more coherence and explicit' (2014, p. 218).

She argues that a translator could add in 'explication or coherence' in order to try to produce a 'comparably obscure text' (2014, pp. 218–9). Obscurity here does not have to mean confusing or incoherent, but rather mysterious, as crime tends to be.

It is clearly a challenge to avoid overexplaining in crime translation, as all the discussion about footnotes, glossaries, obscurity and ambiguity shows. Jenny Brumme writes that 'the reader must infer details and must complete the meaning' and that translators 'tend to explain the hidden signs and to make the cues clearer' (2014, p. 165). As translators are obviously readers first, who must analyse and understand the text before embarking on translating it, this raises a difficulty. Perhaps translators subconsciously clarify certain aspects of the text as they translate, because they know where the plot is heading; this suggests that one possible strategy would be to not read the text before they translate. In other words, they could read each sentence or section at a time in order to retain the suspense for themselves and to thereby not 'make cues clearer' in the target text. On the other hand, some translators may be able to read the text and to avoid letting their knowledge of what is to come influence them.

Finally, as ever, translators must keep in mind not only what the text says – or does not say – but also what their target readers expect of crime novels. Since crime fiction varies depending on the time and place it is written, it is natural that this would impact upon how it is translated. Bradford describes Nordic crime literature as 'mak[ing] full use of the non-Nordic reader's often idealized perception of their society to cause the shattering of expectations to become all the more brutal' (2015, p. 79). This is intriguing in part because it suggests that Nordic writers may be writing with translation in mind, if they are considering the expectations of non-Nordic readers. Whether this is true or not, it does return to the topic of audience expectations. If indeed non-Nordic readers expect a certain type of text from a Nordic author, a translator may feel pressure, perhaps from the publisher of the translated version, to produce that text. What the reader of a crime novel wants from that work may depend on where and when that crime novel was written and/or translated, and this will in turn affect translatorial choices. And, as mentioned, this will thereby reveal and influence ideological perspectives.

Genre 5: Children's Literature

Definitions

Children's literature could be defined as literature written for children or young adults, or, in a more expansive definition, as literature read by children or young adults, whether or not they were the intended audience. One could also attempt to narrow the field in another way; for instance, Riitta Oittinen writes, 'children's books are often illustrated and often meant to be read aloud' (2000, p. 5). But, as with all fields, it is much more complicated than either of those options – that is, defining it based on who reads it or is read it or based on images – with a readership that is far from monolithic.

To understand what literature for children and young adults is, I would suggest that we must first define what a child is. There are multiple ways of doing this, and such definitions vary from culture to culture and over different historical periods. A definition could be based on age, or on the stage of development, for instance. Currently, eighteen is often considered the age of maturity (e.g. UNICEF n.d.), and thus the end of childhood, even though the body is usually physically capable of reproducing in the teenage years before eighteen, while neuroscience has shown that the brain is not fully developed until the mid-twenties. Also, maturity would have to be defined, as many eighteen-year-olds attend university and are still living with parents, at least part of the time, and may be financially supported by parents or government grants; in other words, most do not own their own home and car, work full-time and earn their own money, although we may not wish to define maturity and adulthood on those terms anyway. Childhood may also be differentiated from adulthood by what rights and responsibilities people have or are not yet allowed to have, such as legally being allowed to drink alcohol, or being tried in court, or being able to vote or join the military or to marry; some might consider the lack of rights and responsibilities to mean that this period of time is 'innocent', while others may consider it 'inexperience' instead (Hunt 2009, pp. 13–14).

Naturally, of course, the term 'childhood' covers many years, and a three-year-old would be very different from a sixteen-year-old, while two ten-year-olds could vary wildly in their interests and abilities and have little in common. From this very brief overview of how we might define a child, it becomes clear that actually there are many stages to childhood and that we would need to be more specific about what we were seeking to define. When I ask my students to tell me what a child is, they most often say 'a little person' or 'a young human', as if a child is just a not quite fully fledged adult. When pressed further, they suggest that being in education and not having to work or support a family are the key characteristics, but of course not all children are in full-time education, while some children are carers for others in their family or have to work outside the home, and becoming aware of these facts makes my students realise how Western-centric their understanding of 'child' is.

If the concept of 'child' is so confusing, then so must be the field of children's literature. How can we define a supposed genre if we cannot define its readership? While we generally differentiate between children's literature and young adult literature, it may make sense to break the category down even further, such as by referring to subtypes, including board books, alphabet books, picture books, early readers, middle-grade novels, young adult novels and so on. Or perhaps that is the wrong way to divide what is a very large grouping of texts linked by little more than their young audience. We could, on the contrary, divide works for children according to, well, their genre. There are works for children that can be called science fiction, non-fiction, romance, horror, mystery, family sagas, fairy tales, poetry and much more. This means that what is often considered a genre in and of itself – children's literature – is actually a broad field that contains many genres.

As with the other genres, or categories, explored heretofore, calling a field of disparate works a genre may be done out of ease. Adults in the bookstore or library want to know if a given work is appropriate for the young person they are getting it for. The use of the category or genre name shows consideration for the needs of both the children themselves and the adults who make many of the decisions about what texts children have access to. It is a marketing decision, one that is further emphasised by the use of age bands, those labels on books that specify what age range a book is considered to be for. We do not find such age bands on adult literature – that is, 'This book is appropriate for those in their thirties' – but we do tend to employ them in children's literature, despite knowing how different two children of the same age could be in their development and reading abilities and interests. A number of authors and organisations are against age bands, pointing out that they might embarrass those who need to read an age band that is younger than their actual age or limit those who could read at a higher band but who are held back because the adults in their lives insist they read the supposedly appropriate band (see the No to Age Banding website, n.d.).

Another way of trying to understand children's books is to consider why children read and, thus, what they read. This returns to the point about *skopos*, or function, from earlier in this Element. The function of children's literature has in the past often been considered to be pedagogical, with the aim of books for children being to teach children to read (see Litaudon 2018, pp. 169–79 on ABC books) or which morals to have or how to function in society (see, e.g. Hunt 2009, p. 14). It is only in the past century and a half, and particularly in recent decades, that children's literature, in English at least, has been recognised as an important source of pleasure, as with Lewis Carroll's groundbreaking book *Alice's Adventures in Wonderland* (1865). Books for children may teach them something, but they can, and perhaps ought to, also be enjoyable to read. And they may be enjoyable for both adults and children; children are often read children's books aloud by grown-ups, so works may be aimed at a dual audience and would need to appeal to both groups, and furthermore, readability is essential to consider.

Then there is the question of subject matter and whether children's literature perhaps focusses on issues that are different from literature for adults. For example, Kimberly Reynolds notes that works of children's literature 'will cover key areas such as the adventure, family, school, and animal story, and probably also fantasy, realism, poetry, historical, and war fiction ... the pony story ... the moral tale ... ' (2011, p. 77). This grouping of topics and text types looks like a list of genres – which again challenges the idea that children's literature is a genre in and of itself – but it also suggests a number of topics that might be considered suitable for children's consumption. Reynolds writes about particularly common ones, such as animal stories, which she calls a 'staple genre of children's literature since the 18th century' (2011, p. 81), and family tales, as 'families are ubiquitous in children's literature' (2011, p. 85). On the contrary, there are some topics that are considered unacceptable or inappropriate for children's literature, although this will vary among cultures; the American Library Association's list of challenged and banned books includes many works for children, often for reasons such as homosexuality, violence or a supposed anti-religion attitude. Nonetheless, given that children's literature can contain so many subjects and text types, another possible way of narrowing down a definition might be style. Reynolds writes that

> 'the difference [between adult literature and children's literature] lies less in *what* is written than in *how* stories are told. As a rule, books for children and young adults tend to be vague when referring to potentially disturbing acts or events; readers may fill in the gaps and add details as far as they can or want to, but they are almost never required to confront brutalities or erotica'
>
> (2011, p. 126, emphasis in original).

The suggestion that violence and sex are considered unacceptable in any real detail for young readers relates to the idea that adults are in control of what children consume in book format. While there are always power issues inherent in writing and translation, they are even more prevalent in children's literature. Children's literature is aimed at young people, but it is produced for the most part solely by adults; adults write, illustrate, edit, publish, market, sell, buy, assign and, of course, translate it. On the other hand, literature for adults is produced by adults for other adults. Writers and translators for children must be sure to consider the power they have over young readers, and perhaps over the adults who might be reading books aloud. Riitta Oittinen writes that the 'primary task of the translator for children [is] to think of her/his future readers – children and adults reading aloud to their children' (2000, p. 28). What adults think is suitable for children will vary from culture to culture, with some grown-ups wanting to protect children from certain topics and others believing that young people should have access to any knowledge they are interested in (e.g. Hunt 2009, p. 22).

As this brief overview has shown, anyone who writes or translates for children has a variety of considerations to take account of, including the age and ability of the child reader or read-to, the intended function of the text, questions of appropriateness, style, power and more. I would suggest that adults often overprotect and underestimate children, forgetting both that young people do live in the real world and have the right to know about it and also that young readers, as with older ones, can return to texts and get more from them with each re-reading and as time goes on.

Translation

There are certain issues that, while relevant to other text types as well, are especially pertinent to translating children's literature. Some have been hinted at already, such as the functions of books and how they may be perceived differently in the source and target culture; the dual addressivity of many children's texts, in that they must appeal to both adults and children; or the consideration of the audience, including factors such as the reader or read-to's age, reading level, knowledge, cultural background, version/dialect of language, what is thought to be appropriate or taboo in a given culture and other matters. Another factor is tie-ins and how some books are in a series and/or are adapted from or to TV shows, films or video games, which means that translators may have to work with other translators, subtitlers or larger organisations or industries in other countries in order to find universal solutions to translation issues so that there is consistency throughout a series or between, say, dubbing/subtitling and books.

Some scholars and/or translators have suggested approaches for handling books for young readers. For example, Riitta Oittinen, who was one of the first scholars to write in English about translating for children, has raised the idea of the 'child image'. She writes that 'translators for children are responsible to the author of the original and to the target-language readers, but they are also responsible to themselves as human beings, and to their own child images' (2000, p. 84). By this I think she means in part the child they are translating for, but also their own idea of what a child is. This would inform how translators – and, before them, writers – produce work for children; as the previous section showed, what a child is or is considered to be varies hugely, depending on age, development, culture, historical period, and so forth, so a translator would need to determine their intended child audience before translating. This is not something that is said about translating work for adult readers, which implies that translators have more, or at least different, responsibility towards children and also that translators of work for children and young adults have a potentially more arduous task, because they have to first consider their child image before beginning to translate, and since adults are relatively distanced from childhood, it may be hard to remember being a child or to relate to being a child. They may have to look to children they know now, such as their own or ones they might teach, and to use this to build a child image, which Oittinen says has to take account of the children's 'experiences, abilities, and expectations' (2000, p. 34), but this inevitably would mean making guesses about what a child might know or what might be suitable for the child reader, a topic that comes up frequently in this area of research.

A number of scholars who work on the translation of children's literature, such as Göte Klingberg (1977, 2008), Riitta Oittinen (1993, 2000, 2018), Zohar Shavit (2006), Jan Van Coillie and Walter P. Verschueren (2006) and Gillian Lathey (2006), have explored concepts such as process and product or historical approaches or ideology. The topic of process is particularly useful in this present Element because it relates to strategies or tools. Klingberg, for instance, tends towards the prescriptive; besides suggesting particular strategies (e.g. 1977), he also states that what he calls 'purification', or the removal of taboo elements, may be 'valid' and acceptable when translating for children (2008, p. 15). Zohar Shavit writes, regarding the removal of taboo topics, 'it can even be formulated as a rule that when it is possible to delete undesirable scenes without damaging the basic plot or characterizations, translators will not hesitate to do so' (2006, p. 35). Not all scholars or translators would agree that purification is a 'valid' approach; it is notable that it has not been referred to as a major strategy in reference to other genres, which harkens back to the concept of protecting, or overprotecting, young readers.

Klingberg also writes that it is often necessary to carry out what he terms 'cultural context adaptation' (2008, p. 14). This means taking culturally specific terms or ideas from the source culture and changing them to suit the target culture; Klingberg believes that without such adaptation, the text will be 'more difficult to understand and less interesting' for children (2008, p. 14). Other scholars, such as Lawrence Venuti (1995), as mentioned previously, would call this 'domestication', or making a source text easier for the target reader to comprehend. On the other hand, retaining the original elements is 'foreignization', which can also be said to mean that the target reader has to do more work to come towards the text; foreignization is more likely to be recommended as the strategy for translating adult literature, whereas some theorists, such as Klingberg, believe domestication is necessary because children have less knowledge of cultures beyond their own. This shows that children's literature is viewed differently by some researchers and translators; fidelity – a debatable concept in general in translation – to the words and content may be seen as of higher priority in literature for adults, while consideration of the intended audience's needs can take precedence when it comes to literature for younger readers.

In my own research and my work as a practising translator, I am significantly less prescriptivist, preferring instead for translators to have the freedom and flexibility to make their own decisions on a case-by-case basis. I would suggest that translators will want to carefully consider how a particular word or phrase works and what its function is in the text before coming up with a strategy for how to translate it. Strategies I have discovered in my analysis of the translation of expressive language in children's literature, by which I mean items such as metaphors, wordplay, names, neologisms, allusions and so forth, include retention, replacement, deletion, explanation, adaptation and compensation (2012, pp. 25–6). As an example, a translator may come across a reference to a particular food item that they think would be unfamiliar to readers of the target text as it is unknown in the target culture. Klingberg would likely suggest replacing it, using a similar food item from the target culture instead. Other possibilities would be to add a clarifying word, such as 'pastry' in 'they ate the X pastry' or perhaps using a footnote or glossary to explain the term. Some translators may retain it without explaining it, assuming their audience can figure it out from context or can ask someone or use the internet to look it up if they are unsure. Some might just delete it. Compensation would mean not bothering with this particular reference but instead adding in another one elsewhere. The choice they make depends on what they think the purpose of the food item is in the book and in this particular scene – whether it is important to the story or just a throw-away mention, whether it is meant to educate readers or set the scene, and so forth – and also on how they perceive their intended child audience, in terms of how much knowledge they have about the source culture or context, or how likely they are to make an accurate guess or to ask for help. What I have suggested here for a food item can extend to all sorts of aspects of a text for children, and I do not think it is possible to recommend a universal strategy for handling such words or styles in all works, from all languages to all other languages.

There are several other key points to consider when it comes to work for younger readers. One is readability; this is similar to the speakability or performability discussed in reference to drama. A children's text is often read out loud by grown-ups to young people, and sometimes by children who are learning to read and are expected to read aloud to parents or teachers. Children's books, in other words, are frequently performative in a way that other texts are not necessarily (except for drama and poetry, among a few others). Oittinen, as already cited, discusses reading aloud as the key feature (2000, p. 28), and this would mean thinking about rhythm and rhyme and how words work together. It is, in most cases, impossible to retain everything about the style, content, word choices and sound of the words when translating, so here some level of adaptation and prioritising is inevitable. Some translators, myself included, choose to read their drafts aloud to children in order to get feedback from the intended audience. Other translators may work together and read drafts aloud to one another, while still others may record themselves reading aloud and then analyse the recording (Lathey 2015, p. 94). There are also issues of readability regarding dialects, idiolects and child language; while some of this has been discussed in terms of other genres already, what is important to note here in particular is that translators may worry about child readers not knowing the dialects or not understanding the connotations or stereotypes meant to be associated with the given dialects, or they may be concerned with the messages children get from this non-standard language usage (e.g. Lathey 2015, pp. 75–90, and Epstein 2012, pp. 197–238). Still, translators must make choices, and strategies can include using their own form of language or another particular dialect, among other possibilities.

Another characteristic that makes children's books different from those for adults is the illustrations. Picture books and many other words for children contain images, and the images themselves might contain text, which would likely require translation, but even more importantly, translators have to consider the relationship between words and images in the text. In a picture book, for example, there are images and there are usually words (except for wordless books; see Bosch 2018, pp. 191–200) and they each have their meaning, and meanwhile there is the relationship between the two and how they may tell a story together that is greater than the sum of the individual parts (cf. Nodelman 1988). As publishers cannot always afford to commission new illustrations if the translator suggests doing so in order to retain the same content, this means the translator may have to change the text (cf. Oittinen 2018, pp. 463–70). For instance, in *Alice Through the Looking-Glass* by Lewis Carroll, there is reference to a 'bread-and-butterfly' (2000, p. 173), an obvious play on the English insect name butterfly and on the dessert bread-and-butter pudding. The illustration by John Tenniel shows this new creature. This could not be translated easily, because a butterfly does not necessarily have a name with a reference to butter or another food item in every language. Tenniel is not alive and could not produce a new image of another insect to suit whatever a translator came up with and, as noted, a publisher might not be able to get a new image to fit the translation or might not find an illustrator with a style similar to Tenniel's. Gillian Lathey writes that possible strategies for translating the visual include 'altering or repositioning existing artwork' (2015, p. 56) and also suggests that commissioning new images is 'common practice in the case of retranslations of classics or of fairy tales' (2015, p. 57). Whether a given work is viewed as a classic and whether a publisher would want to commission new images depends on the circumstances and in regard to 'altering or repositioning', this may not help in the case of a visual pun. So a translator will have to either ignore the image – which would affect how to reader understands the word-image connection and may puzzle the reader and change the story – or come up with an insect name that suits the bread-and-butter-based image but that perhaps is not a butterfly and thus does not fit the picture (see Epstein 2013, p.185). As is often the case, it is a question of functions, priorities and knowledge, and each translator and publisher would have their own assumptions and views about those things in relation to the intended audience.

Previous sections questioned identity politics – for example, whether one must be LGBTQ+ to translate LGBTQ+ literature or a woman or a feminist to translate women's writing – and as all adults have been children, here the question could be whether one must have children of one's own in order to translate for children; the concept of the 'child image' is not the same thing. While current views in translation studies are descriptivist rather than prescriptivist, which means that it cannot be firmly claimed that a translator must have children in order to translate for young people, it seems obvious from the foregoing review of research in the field that translators need some knowledge of and connection to young people. It may be that memories of their own childhood could be enough or else they could read widely in children's literature in both the source and the target language to construct an idea about how people write for children in the two cultures.

I believe that one of the biggest concerns here is in regard to translators and publishers underestimating children – as some earlier scholars mentioned here were wont to do – and thereby purifying and changing books for children more than necessary. We cannot assume that children need everything explained to them or that they cannot handle learning about people with differing views or experiences or that they are too 'innocent' to be told what the world is really like. Meeting children where they are, or perhaps expecting a little too much from them and allowing them to rise to meet the book, is, I would argue, the ideal way to translate for them and to avoid abusing our power over them.

Genre 6: Science Fiction

Definitions

David Seed begins his book about science fiction by writing, 'Science fiction has proved notoriously difficult to define' (2011, p. 1). This, of course, puts it in good company with each of the other so-called genres I discuss in this Element, in that they have all been challenging to define and seem to evade easy categorisation. Seed goes on to say that 'to call science fiction (SF) a genre causes problems because it does not recognize the hybrid nature of many SF works. It is more helpful to think of it as a mode or field where different genres and subgenres intersect' (2011, p. 1). This, too, has been true of all the other genres or modes explored already. Seed concludes his attempted definition of science fiction by noting that it 'is about the writer's present in the sense that any historical moment will include its own set of expectations and perceived tendencies. The futures represented in SF embody its speculative dimension' (2011, pp. 1–2). The references to expectations and perceptions are not a surprise at this stage, in view of the fact that so many fields appear to be defined by writer and reader (and publisher, editor, translator, bookseller, teacher, etc.) expectations and beliefs.

In an anthology on science fiction, Roger Luckhurst gives up on attempting a definition and refers to 'looseness and improvisations', calling this a 'liberation from artificial [genre] boundaries' (2017, p. 10). And yet, if one is going to have a book on science fiction – or a book that is called science fiction – one must need some sort of understanding of what that even means. Arthur B. Evans explains how science fiction is seen as a multitude of different things by different people; some label work SF only if it 'contain[s] extrapolated scientific content, or … recount[s] the adventures and events resulting from a specific, imagined scientific breakthrough', while others call it 'a kind of thought experiment that examines some version of reality', and still others employ 'narratological and linguistic theory to demonstrate the genre's unique ways of signifying', and some define it subjectively, feeling they know it if they see it, or that it is SF if they label it so (2017, p. 12). Evans goes on to say firmly that 'SF does exist' but now 'traditionally understood SF may meld and overlap with fantasy, horror, surrealism and other literary genres, and for some critics, the very notion of a single 'genre' has become increasingly suspect' (2017, p. 12). Seed tries to sum up the definitions by arguing that 'repeated attempts to redefine or redescribe itself are integral to SF as it progressively tries to situate itself in the literary market place' (2011, p. 117); this relates to marketing and reader expectations, as well as emphasises the importance of fluidity in genre definitions. Still, despite the defining and redefining, what links most of these possible understandings of science fiction seems to be in the title of the genre itself: science and fiction, a blend of the true and the not-true, or, perhaps more accurately, the true and the not-yet-true.

Mark Bould and Sherryl Vint discuss competing histories for science fiction, which relates to definitions. They write that some people consider science fiction to have 'originat[ed] in 1920s American pulps' and that this understanding of the field emphasises the importance of the fans, including conventions and fanzines (2011, pp. 5–6). This view of science fiction considers it to be a form of literature that combines prophecies about the future with contemporary scientific understanding. The second definition, which stems from the scholar Darko Suvin's work in the late 1970s, explores science fiction as 'a literature premised upon a radical discontinuity from the empirical world, but whose features' are potentially possible (2011, p. 17). Bould and Vint seem to argue that Suvin has titled a genre opposed to realistic fiction as science fiction and that this is rather different from the way science fiction was understood in the five decades before his work (2011, p. 17). They write that his 'insistence that SF must have a critical relationship to the social world contemporary to its production defines the genre in terms not of specific textual features or content but of its ability to promote social change' (2011, p. 17), and this links to the emphasis in some SF on utopias and dystopias (e.g. Seed 2011, pp. 73–96), or the idea of exploring the world as it should be. As Bould and Vint note, Suvin's view also means there is less emphasis on the role of the fans or on paperbacks and so forth (Seed 2011, pp. 73–96). In other words, there seem to be two genres, or modes, called science fiction, one of which could perhaps be considered more speculative as well as fan-based, while the other looks to enact changes in the world as it is today; it is interesting that a single critic has had such an apparent influence on one genre. However, both of these histories seem very centred in the United States and focussed on English-language literature.

Not all scholars agree with this divided interpretation of this type of literature. Seed writes that '[o]ne of the first images we associate with science fiction is the spaceship' and trips to space, so he argues that based on this understanding of science fiction, there have been SF works since the seventeenth century (2011, p. 6), referring to Cyrano de Bergerac's French-language narratives. Other scholars go even further back; Evans mentions ancient Greek myths or Sir Thomas More's *Utopia* from the sixteenth century as possible early science fiction works (2017, p. 13). Interestingly, given the focus of this Element, I found few specific mentions to the role of translation in the shaping of science fiction as a literary field; while many modern SF books are written in English, clearly others have been translated to English and would have influenced how science fiction was viewed, or how the field or genre developed.

In terms of characteristics of the genre, several have already been named, such as the desire to effect change in society, the involvement of fans, the depiction of science and scientific advancements, space voyages and so on. Seed also writes that SF has 'a refreshing tendency to self-parody' (2011, p. 7). He further states that early SF used 'three main settings: the Earth itself, near space, and the interior of the Earth' (2011, p. 8), which suggests the importance of location, particularly space; later, actual space exploration inspired further SF based in and around space (e.g. Seed 2011, p. 21). Space then, understandably, lends itself as a location for battles, space wars or 'space operas' (Seed 2011, p. 12), and, furthermore, as a setting for interactions with aliens. As Seed writes, 'aliens in science fiction are by definition always imagined through reference to familiar human groups, animal species, or machines' (2011, p. 28). They are also seen through historical lenses. Besides space being the location for alien encounters, aliens may invade earth; Seed explains that this became common after World War 2 – for the obvious reason that people became more concerned about invasions, conquests and extermination – and that aliens then were seen in SF as 'creatures whose actions were presented as invasive and threatening' (2011, p. 31). Gender was previously discussed in relation to crime fiction, but it is important to note that women have frequently been absent from science fiction or have been embodied in the role of the alien: '[t]he SF hero was traditionally male and women tended to have marginal and conventional roles, or were represented as 'other', with their difference embodied within the figure of the alien' (Bianchi 2018, p. 902). Bould and Vint agree that 'SF's fascination with artificial beings, such as robots, and non-human lifeforms, whether terrestrial or alien, often articulates an interest in questions of class, race, gender and sexuality' (2011, p. 39).

One of the most important aspects of science fiction is surely technology. Bould and Vint write that '[a]lthough the specific role of science in SF is a contentious one, SF texts do typically engage with science and technology in various ways, ranging from the adventures they enable to the detailed exploration of a scientific premise' (2011, p. 39). And Seed writes that '[o]ne of the most recurrent themes in science fiction is its examination of humanity's relation to its own material constructions, sometimes to celebrate progress, sometimes in a more negative spirit of ... technophobia, through fictions articulating fears of human displacement' (2011, p. 47). He adds that '[t]echnology is a central indicator of change in science fiction' (2011, p. 47). In other words, what technology has already developed or could be developed influences how SF authors write about the world as it is and as it could be, and scientific advances can be viewed with excitement, suspicion or any other mix of emotions. Spaceships have already been mentioned as a form of technology to frequently feature in SF, and other types of technology include robots and cyborgs (Seed 2011, pp. 59–64), computers (Seed 2011, pp. 65–8), and more, but Seed argues that '[t]he city is the supreme embodiment of technological construction, and for this reason science fiction has been a heavily urban literary mode' (2011, p. 52).

A final key characteristic of science fiction is time. Seeds writes that '[m]ore than any other literary mode, science fiction is closely associated with the future, in other words with time under its different aspects. It is above all a literature of change, and change by definition implies that the present is perceived in relation to perceptions of the past and expectations of the future which shape the present' (2011, p. 97). Science fiction, then, is likely to consider time as a subject and to take place in the future – if it were in the past, it would often be called historical fiction, although there is some science fiction set in the past (see Seed 2011, p. 99) – and to reflect on what might happen, such as in a post-nuclear world (see Seed 2011, pp. 105–10), or to explore alternate histories (see Seed 2011, pp. 110–13), or to try to effect changes, as Suvin argues.

There is obviously much flexibility in the field of science fiction in terms of what people write and how they write, with a few common links seen in many, but not all, SF texts, such as technology, time and space. If science fiction comments on the world as it could or should be, then this will be dependent on the time and culture that a particular text is being produced in, so a text will invariably have different associations depending on the readership.

Translation

When Bould and Vint write that science fiction 'exists as a fuzzily-edged, multidimensional and constantly shifting discursive object' (2011, p. 5), this suggests to me that translators will likewise need 'multidimensional and constantly shifting' approaches to translating it. If it is not straightforward to understand what science fiction as a whole is or what its characteristics are, then it is unlikely to be clear-cut to suggest translation strategies. To make it even more complicated, some view 'language as a form of technology, and translation as a possible meta-technology' (Hanff 2020, p. 5), which perhaps would question whether it is even possible to translate science fiction. The conclusion William A. Hanff comes to, at least, is that it is in fact possible to translate science fiction, but that translation itself is a form of science fiction because it 'explor[es] the inexactitude of language [and is] a form of phenomenology shared between the two thinkers' (2020, p. 7). This may be freeing, in that translators need not worry about the 'inexactitude' of their translations and may choose to feel that what they are doing is helping to communicate a text and its ideas between the author and the target reader.

That being said, some scholars have nonetheless found more specific approaches for translating science fiction. Jiali Gao and Yan Hua, for instance, focus on the interaction between the science and the fiction. They write that '[u]nlike ordinary literary genres, science fiction involves both scientific and technological knowledge and literariness, which makes it a challenge for translators' (2021, p. 187). In a somewhat prescriptive manner, they write that it 'should contain literariness, which should be reflected in the description of characters, environment, psychological activities', should have a 'strong personal style', should be 'popular', and also has a need 'to abide by scientific conclusions' (2021, p. 187). They say the latter is important because '[n]o matter how fanciful the author is, the world he creates must be based on scientific laws. Otherwise, it will violate the requirements of science fiction' (2021, p. 187). So this combination of things makes it a challenge, which Gao and Hua acknowledge, although they also seem to feel that it is clear what the translator should do: 'The translation is a multilingual interaction, and it is sometimes difficult for us to cover all bases. Different cultural backgrounds and logical thinking will bring challenges to translators. What the translators should do is to communicate the content of the original text to the target readers as much as possible and help the readers to understand it in an easy-to-understand way' (2021, p. 187). They appear to be of the opinion that the scientific aspects should be prioritised because they write that '[t]ranslators should particularly pay attention to the accuracy of terminology translation and ensure that the text is well-knit and logical' (2021, p. 187). This almost makes translating SF sound like technical translation.

Gao and Hua survey other research on translation strategies for science fiction, and list them as follows: 'footnotes or in-text annotations to explain cultural words and provide readers with background information' (2021, p. 186), and 'literal translation, free translation, transliteration, and addition' (2021, p. 186). You Wu also emphasises the use of footnotes and annotations, as a way of explaining and 'both preserv[ing] the exotic cultural flavour [of the original] and ensur[ing] a pleasant reading experience for the target-language readers' (2020, p. 61). Footnotes or in-text explanations have rarely been looked upon in a positive manner for the other genres discussed in this Element, usually because they are seen as taking the reader out of the world of the text; my speculative reasons to explain why they are recommended for science fiction are because a) these scholars seem to mostly be focussing on Chinese translations, and it may be considered more standard in Chinese literature to annotate, or b) science fiction is seen as unrealistic already, or c) SF is thought to need more explanation, especially on its journey from one language to another, so adding a footnote, explanation or annotation is not viewed as something that will bother the average reader. I have no firm evidence for any of these explanations, however. Diana Bianchi finds that paratextual material can be employed in translations of science fiction for other reasons, besides explaining technical details; she writes, 'it is at the paratextual level that some interesting interpretive elements can be observed – i.e. in the editorials and introductions' and what these interpretive elements do is raise awareness of the feminist, or potentially misogynist, elements of the text (2018, p. 904). As was discussed earlier about women's fiction, feminist translation strategies aim to force readers to consider gender when reading a text, and Bianchi suggests that there may be reason to do this in the formerly quite male territory of science fiction.

In terms of the other strategies, Gao and Hua go on to explain that free translation may be appropriate because, for popular fiction in general and science fiction more specifically, 'it is necessary to make the translation easy to understand and maintain the balance between popularity and literariness. This requires translators to have a correct understanding of the text first, and then to translate and facilitate the target audience to understand' (2021, p. 188). Free translation, in their view, would allow translators of science fiction to focus on adapting the text as necessary so readers can understand it, even if this means changing intended meanings.

But the approach they suggest for the scientific aspects of the text is different; here, they feel literal translation is the right choice because '[s]cience fiction needs to be scientific, so translators need to carefully consider the translation of these scientific terms to ensure that the articles are well-knit and congenial with scientific knowledge' (2021, pp. 188–9). For neologisms, on the other hand, Gao and Hua write that literal translation may sometimes work, but that transcreation may be the better approach, allowing a translator to replicate terms invented by the author. Goa and Hua, influenced by Wilhelm von Humboldt, write,

> 'The creativity of language reflects the idea that human beings have unlimited thinking. Although the rules of language are limited, human beings can make unlimited use of them. This creativity can be divided into regular creation and irregular creation according to whether it depends on previous experience and rules or not. Therefore, we can get two translation methods: word-formation based on existing words and derivation' (2021, p. 189).

While Gao and Hua appear rather prescriptive in their suggestions, they do also admit that 'the creation and translation of science fiction are complementary' (2021, p. 190), by which they seem to mean that both are creative tasks that demand flexibility on the part of the author and translator. They feel that the more technology-based aspects of the texts need clear explanations and literal translations, but that there is room for translators to adapt and create as necessary otherwise. You Wu agrees with this and even goes a little further, writing 'literary translation is comparable to artistic creation, in which process an outstanding translator can make up for the limited nature of the original work in certain situations, endowing the source text with a new life' (2020, p. 60). This implies that a translator can feel free to improve upon a text; Wu even describes a translator of science fiction as a 'promoter' (2020, p. 60), which suggests a heavier level of responsibility than that seen in some of the other genres explored in this Element.

Discussing translations of Jules Verne, who some consider to be a science fiction writer, Bould and Vint write that '[t]ranslation inevitably alters nuance and connotation' and they note that early Verne translations were 'often poor and incomplete' and yet they shaped what science fiction was understood by some people to be (2011, p. 11). Furthermore, they state that 'SF is proliferating globally across media' now (2011, p. 202). Undoubtedly, the translation of texts matters, and can impact how an entire genre, or mode, is viewed and how others come to write it, while also sharing ideas across linguistic and cultural borders.

It seems that scholars suggest both more explanation – more literalness, more adherence to the scientific – as well as more freedom – more flexibility, more creativity around the fictional aspects when it comes to translating science fiction. This may seem paradoxical and tricky, but perhaps that is exactly what science fiction requires.

Conclusion

In this Element, I have tried to explore the idea of genre generally and specific genres and their translation in more detail. It would be impossible to try to categorise all genres and to cover them in depth in one work; for example, genres that have not been discussed here include – or may include, depending on how we define genre – Gothic writing, Christian books, vampire literature, romance, epics, poems, graphic novels, bildungsroman, fantasy, horror, travel writing, memoirs, comedy, historical fiction, Westerns, fairy tales, myths and so forth. I recognise, in other words, that I provided only a limited selection here. Despite this, I think this was a productive, if subjective, grouping of genres, which served in some ways to reveal how complex the term is.

In the foregoing, I have cited or myself used a variety of words that are often conflated with genre, such as mode, field, style, category, system and text type. Beyond that, I have discussed subgenres, generic features, functions of genres or specific texts and more. After all this, can we actually answer the question: What is genre?

Genre is a set of suppositions, expectations, conventions, processes and/or values that is situated in a particular cultural and historical context. It can be seen as a shortcut, helping authors to know how to write a particular type of text, or assisting readers to choose works that they might enjoy, or providing translators with tools for transforming the book into another language. But, as shown earlier, it is much more complicated than a simple list of rules and there is much bleeding between boundaries. This suggests that we should not consider generic labels to be written in stone, to use a cliché; they are not as clear-cut and unyielding as some believe. In fact, Bould and Vint write that '[g]enres are best thought of as ongoing processes of negotiation rather than fixed entities that pre-exist their naming' (2011, p. 1). They are fluid, with changing dimensions, and changing perceptions given the time and place where they exist; '[o]nly history reminds us how contingent any particular identification actually is' (Owen, 2007, p. 1393). Despite the changing nature of genre, there are clearly certain expectations and features that go with most genres or types or categories.

Stephen Owen, acknowledging the changeable nature and intrinsic instability in genres, writes, '[t]he actual world of literary texts is a mass of family resemblances, shared terms, and analogies. The putatively complete set of categories is a sorting mechanism to privilege one level of resemblances over others and give us the illusion of knowledge. The fate of such sets is well known: sets proliferate with new categories, subsets, and hierarchies; they are inherently unstable' (2007, p. 1392). Bould and Vint argue that genres 'are the discursive product of enrolment processes undertaken by numerous actants with different, and at times conflicting, agendas' (2011, p. 19). I do not fully agree with this, because this suggests that genres are defined, in as much as they are or can be defined, by the authors and texts considered to fall under that particular genre heading; there is also the question of who 'enrols' the works in the genre category and why. Still, while that is certainly one way of looking at it, I think it is more productive to consider it from a broader scope, not just looking at texts and authors but also thinking about readers, publishers, translators, booksellers, librarians, teachers and the market more generally.

Indeed, while labelling a work as belonging to a particular genre can positively impact how a writer writes, an editor edits, a translator translates, a publisher publishes and markets, a bookseller sells, a librarian promotes, a teacher teaches and a reader reads by suggesting ways of shaping their process and their understanding, it can also have an adverse limiting effect. For instance, it can mean that certain elements of a text are smoothed over or removed or, if they remain, they might be considered experimental or out of place. A text can be underestimated – or overestimated – due to its label, and thus not seen for what it really is. I would suggest that we continue to use genres with caution and to try to look beyond the terms in order to see what sort of text we actually have. This relates back to an idea mentioned at the beginning of this Element, namely that humans have a need and a use for categorising and labelling and that we use differentiations in part as a way of knowing who and what is safe versus dangerous. While this can serve us well, it can also cause problems, because it can lead us to stereotype or make assumptions about a person or a thing, simply from knowing what category it belongs to. Categories are not always accurate and a label does not always provide us with all the information we require.

Genres contain genres, or texts can be beyond genres, and genres are ever-evolving based on the texts perceived to be 'members' of those categories; translators, thus, must be prepared to work with the text they have before them to the best of their ability, without making too many assumptions about what sort of text it is, but while also retaining awareness of authorial intentions and audience expectations. Expectations – a term mentioned repeatedly throughout this Element– is probably the key concept: genre is about both the audience expectations and expectations of the audience. In other words, writers, publisher and translators have to consider who they think will read the work and why along with what they think readers will know or understand or want. Translating a work perceived as belonging to a particular genre is, one could say, about managing expectations and adhering to conventions to a certain extent.

A translator will need to consider the intended or actual functions of a given text type and a specific text within that type in both the source and target languages and cultures. They will also have to analyse the textual features in order to consider appropriate strategies for achieving the same effects in translation. Examples of features mentioned in this Element have included dialect, ambiguity, stage directions, depictions of genders, technology and much more. While many researchers, myself included, have found particular strategies being employed and also often even define and recommend certain approaches, it is also clear that there is no one right way for translating any text or any genre. Each text has to be seen as an individual, rather than as something that necessarily adheres to perceived conventions, and thus each translator may want and need to consider the genre and the generic conventions but will also necessarily have to find strategies that work for the particular text in front of them as well as tactics that suit the circumstances in which they are working.

But how much power and freedom do translators really have? Von Flotow argues that

> 'the translator (and the team made up of editor, copy editor, revisor, pub-
> lisher) have considerable leeway in how they prepare and present a text for
> a new readership. Not only can the choice of text be made from a socio-
> critical standpoint, but the translation itself can reflect and draw attention to
> aspects of the source text that are new, or innovative, or deemed 'useful' for
> the new readership' (2011, p. 7).

As a practising translator myself, I do not always feel I have that 'leeway' and power; editors and publishers make final decisions, and may override my choices and ignore my explanations about those choices. But I do agree that we can produce translations that can 'reflect and draw attention' to particular aspects of the text and its genre, or genres, and to thereby raise awareness of, challenge or expand ideas of literature, including genres.

As this Element has shown, we use genre labels, despite knowing how fluid and ever-changing these categories are, and we use them in part as a sort of shorthand. They guide the work that writers, translators and readers do, but there is often also room to challenge or push against generic conventions and guidelines. Translators work both within and without the genre labels. Owen writes that, '[i]n reading a text, we "identify" or "recognize" a genre. If we attempt to define or describe a genre as such, we are engaging in an entirely different order of activity, one remarkably close to legislation or border control' (2007, p. 1389). Translators are, by definition, people working between and outside of borders; border control is not what we do. Translators break down borders by making texts and ideas available in a new language and by challenging perceived notions, including definitions of what genres might or might not be. We cannot be rigid in our adherence to an understanding of genres or else our translations may not work in the target culture.

In sum, genre is both a help and a hindrance; it may limit expectations and options, although this in and of itself sometimes can spark creativity. Such limits can also help guide the work of a translator. Genre is a border, but it is also a border that is meant to be crossed.

References

Aaltonen, S. (2000). *Time-Sharing on Stage*. Clevedon: Multilingual Matters.

Alvstad, C. (2018). Children's Literature. In K. Washbourne and B. Van Wyke, eds., *The Routledge Handbook of Literary Translation*. Abingdon, UK: Routledge, pp. 159–80.

American Library Association (2021). Banned and Challenged Books. www.ala.org/advocacy/bbooks.

Angles, J. (2017). Queer Translation/Translating Queer in Japan. In B. J. Epstein and R. Gillett, eds., *Queer in Translation*. Abingdon, UK: Routledge, pp. 87–103.

Appalachian State University (2019). Mystery and Crime Fiction: Genres. https://guides.library.appstate.edu/c.php?g=65444&p=422034.

Apter, E. (2007). Taskography: Translation as Genre of Literary Labor. *Publications of the Modern Language Association*, 122(5), pp. 1403–15.

Baer, B. J. (2017). A Poetics of Evasion: The Queer Translations of Aleksei Apukhtin. In B. J. Epstein and R. Gillett, eds., *Queer in Translation*. Abingdon, UK: Routledge, pp. 51–63.

Bauer, H., ed. (2015). *Sexology and Translation: Cultural and Scientific Encounters Across the Modern World*. Philadelphia, PA: Temple University Press.

Bawarshi, A. S. and Reiff, M. J. (2010). *Genre: An Introduction to History, Theory, Research, and Pedagogy*. Anderson, SC: Parlor Press.

Beebee, T. O. (1994). *The Ideology of Genre*. University Park: The Pennsylvania State University Press.

Bennett, A. and Royle, R. (1960/2014). *An Introduction to Literature, Criticism and Theory*, 4th ed. Abingdon, UK: Routledge.

Bianchi, D. (2018). Dangerous Visions? The Circulation and Translation of Women's Crime Fiction and Science Fiction. *Perspectives*, 26(6), pp. 901–15.

Bloom, H. (1994). *The Western Canon: The Books and School of the Ages*. New York: Harcourt Brace.

Bloom, P. (2010). *How Pleasure Works*. London: Random House.

Boase-Beier, J. (2019). *Translation and Style*, 2nd ed. London: Taylor & Francis.

Boehm, P. (2001). Some Pitfalls of Translating Drama. *Translation Review*, 62(1), pp. 27–9. http://doi.org/10.1080/07374836.2001.10523796.

Bosch, E. (2018). Wordless Picturebooks. In B. Kümmerling-Meibauer, ed., *The Routledge Companion to Picturebooks*. Abingdon, UK: Routledge, pp. 191–200.

Bould, M. and Vint, S. (2011). *The Routledge Concise History of Science Fiction*. Abingdon, UK: Routledge.

Bradford, R. (2015). *Crime Fiction: A Very Short Introduction*. Oxford: Oxford University Press.

Brennan, S. (2016). *The Argonauts* by Maggie Nelson (review). *Kennedy Institute of Ethics Journal*, 26(3), pp. 19–22.

Brodie, G. (2017). *The Translator on Stage*. London: Bloomsbury.

Brodie, G. (2018). Performing the Literal: Translating Chekhov's *Seagull* for the Stage. In J. Boase-Beier, L. Fisher, H. Furukawa, eds., *The Palgrave Handbook of Literary Translation*. London: Palgrave, pp. 209–29. https://doi .org/10.1007/978-3-319-75753-7_11.

Brumme, J. (2014). The Narrator's Voice in Translation: What Remains from a Linguistic Experiment in Wolf Hass's Brenner Detective Novels. In S. M. Cadera and A. P. Pintarić, eds., *The Voices of Suspense and Their Translation in Thrillers*. Amsterdam: Rodopi, pp. 161–76.

Burton, W. M. (2010). Inverting the Text: A Proposed Queer Translation Praxis. *In Other Words: Translating Queers/Queering Translation*, B.J. Epstein, ed., 36, pp. 54–68.

Cadera, S. M. and Pintarić, A. P., eds. (2014). *The Voices of Suspense and Their Translation in Thrillers*. Amsterdam: Rodopi .

Cambridge Dictionary (n.d.). Drama. https://dictionary.cambridge.org/diction ary/english/drama.

Carlson, M. (2014). *Theatre: A Very Short Introduction*. Oxford: Oxford University Press.

Carroll, L. (1865/2001). *The Annotated Alice*. London: Penguin.

Castro, O. and Ergun, E. (2018). Translation and Feminism. In J. Evans and F. Fernandez, eds., *The Routledge Handbook of Translation and Politics*. Abingdon, UK: Routledge, pp. 125–44.

Collins, K. (2019). The Morbidity of Maternity: Radical Receptivity in Maggie Nelson's *The Argonauts*. *Criticism*, 61(3), pp. 311–34.

Conacher, A. (2006). Susanne de Lotbinière-Harwood: Totally Between. In A. Whitfield, ed. *Writing Between the Lines*. Waterloo, ON: Wilfrid Laurier University Press, pp. 245–66.

Davis, W. (2007). Am I a Gay Writer? *The Guardian*, 3 July. www .theguardian.com/books/booksblog/2007/jul/03/amiagaywriter.

Dimock, W. C. (2007). Introduction: Genres as Fields of Knowledge. *Publications of the Modern Language Association*, 122(5), pp. 1377–88.

Edgar, D. (2009). *How Plays Work*. London: Nick Hern Books.

Epstein, B. J., ed. (2010). *In Other Words: Translating Queers/Queering Translation*, 36.

Epstein, B. J. (2011). Girl with the Dragon Translation: Translating Thrillers and Thrilling Translations. *FIT XIX Congress Proceedings*.

Epstein, B. J. (2012) *Translating Expressive Language in Children's Literature*. Bern: Peter Lang.

Epstein, B. J. (2013). *Are the Kids All Right? Representations of LGBTQ Characters in Children's and Young Adult Literature*. Bristol: Hammer On Press.

Epstein, B. J. (2017). Eradicalisation: Eradicating the Queer in Children's Literature. In B. J. Epstein and R. Gillett, eds., *Queer in Translation*. Abingdon, UK: Routledge, pp. 118–28.

Epstein, B. J. and Gillett, R., eds. (2017). *Queer in Translation*. Abingdon, UK: Routledge.

Evans, A. B. (2017). The Beginnings: Early Forms of Science Fiction. In R. Luckhurst, ed., *Science Fiction: A Literary History*. London: The British Library, pp. 11–43.

Feral, A. L. (2011). Sexuality and Femininity in Translated Chick Texts. In L. von Flotow, ed., *Translating Women*. Ottawa: University of Ottawa Press, pp. 183–202.

Flood, A. (2021a). Winterson on 'Wimmins' Fiction. *The Guardian*, 12 June.

Flood, A. (2021b). First Woman to Translate Arabian Nights Strips Out Racism and Sexism. *The Guardian*, 16 December. www.theguardian.com/books/ 2021/dec/15/new-arabian-nights-translation-to-strip-away-earlier-versions- racism-and-sexism.

Frow, J. (2006). *Genre*. Abingdon: Routledge.

Galo, S. (2016). What Is Women's Writing? Publishing Insiders Discuss Power of Female Voices. *The Guardian*, 13 September. www.theguardian.com /books/2016/sep/13/womens-writing-publishing-industry-emily-books.

Gao, J. and Hua, Y. (2021). On the English Translation Strategy of Science Fiction from Humboldt's Linguistic Worldview – Taking the English Translation of Three-Body Problem as an Example. *Theory and Practice in Language Studies*, 11(2), pp. 186–90.

Gardiner, J. K. (1981). On Female Identity and Writing by Women. *Critical Inquiry*, 8(2), pp. 347–61.

Gledhill, C. and Ball, V. (1997/2013). Genre and Gender: The Case of Soap Opera. In S. Hall, J. Evans and S. Nixon, eds., *Representation*, 2nd ed. London: Sage, pp. 335–84.

Hanff, W. A. (2020). Fiktions des Wissenschaft – Is Science Fiction Translatable? Or is Translation a Science Fiction? *Flusser Studies*, 30(1). www.flusserstudies.net/archive/flusser-studies-30-november-2020-vil%C3%A9m-flusser-and-his-%E2%80%9Clanguages%E2%80%9D.

Harvey, K. (1998). Translating Camp Talk. *The Translator*, 4(2), pp. 295–320.

Henderson, L. (2018). Why Our Brains See the World as 'Us' versus 'Them'. *The Conversation*, 22 June. www.scientificamerican.com/article/why-our-brains-see-the-world-as-us-versus-them/.

Henitiuk, V. (1999). Translating Woman: Reading the Female through the Male. *Meta*, 44(3), pp. 469–84. https://doi.org/10.7202/003045ar.

Holligan, A. (2021). Why a White Poet Did Not Translate Amanda Gorman. *BBC News*, 10 March. www.bbc.co.uk/news/world-europe-56334369.

Hunt, P. (2009). Instruction and Delight. In J. Maybin and N. J. Watson, eds., *Children's Literature: Approaches and Territories*. Hampshire: Palgrave Macmillan, pp. 12–25.

James, P. D. (2009). *Talking about Detective Fiction*. Oxford: Bodleian Library.

Johnson, J. (2020). Number of Books Sold in the UK from 2009 to 2018. *Statista*, 5 March. www.statista.com/statistics/261278/number-of-books-sold-in-the-uk/.

Klingberg, G. (1977). *Att Översätta Barn- och Ungdomsböcker* [Translating Children's and Young Adults' Books]. Gothenburg, Sweden: Pedagogiska institutionen, Lärarhögskolan i Göteborg.

Klingberg, G. (2008). *Facets of Children's Literature Research*. Stockholm: Swedish Institute for Children's Books.

Komporaly, J. (2021). Translating Hungarian Drama for the British and the American Stage. Hungarian Cultural Studies. *e-Journal of the American Hungarian Educators Association*, 14, pp. 164–75. http://ahea.pitt.edu, http://doi.org/10.5195/ahea.2021.434.

Kümmerling-Meibauer, B., ed. (2018). *The Routledge Companion to Picturebooks*. Abingdon, UK: Routledge.

Oxford Reference. (2021). Lad Lit. www.oxfordreference.com/view/10.1093/oi/authority.20110803100047415.

Lathey, G., ed. (2006). *The Translation of Children's Literature*. Clevedon: Multilingual Matters.

Lathey, G. (2015). *Translating Children's Literature*. Abingdon, UK: Routledge.

Leone, L. (2014). Reconstructing Suspense: Borges Translates Faulkner's The Wild Palms. In S. M. Cadera and A. P. Pintarić, eds., *The Voices of Suspense and Their Translation in Thrillers*. Rodopi: Amsterdam, pp. 77–91.

Lew, E. S. (2010). 'This Is My Girlfriend, Linda': Translating Queer Relationships in Film. *In Other Words: Translating Queers/Queering Translation*, B.J. Epstein, ed., 36, pp. 3–22.

Linder, D. (2014). Chester Himes's *For Love of Imabelle* in Spanish: Josep Elias's 'Absurdly' Overcompensated Slang. In S. M. Cadera and A. P. Pintarić, eds., *The Voices of Suspense and Their Translation in Thrillers*. Rodopi: Amsterdam, pp. 95–110.

Litaudon, M.-P. (2018). ABC Books. In B. Kümmerling-Meibauer, ed., *The Routledge Companion to Picturebooks*. Abingdon, UK: Routledge, pp. 169–79.

Luckhurst, R. (2017). Introduction. In R. Luckhurst, ed., *Science Fiction: A Literary History*. London: The British Library, pp. 8–10.

Luckhurst, R. ed. (2017). *Science Fiction: A Literary History*. London: The British Library.

Maier, C. (1998). Issues in the Practice of Translating Women's Fiction. *Bulletin of Hispanic Studies*, 75(1), pp. 95–108.

Mandel, E. (1984). *Delightful Murder*. London: Pluto Press.

Massardier-Kenney, F. (1997). Towards a Redefinition of Feminist Translation Practice. *The Translator*, 3(1), pp. 55–69.

Moffett, M. W. (2013). Human Identity and the Evolution of Societies. *Human Nature*, 24(3), pp. 219–67.

Munday. J. (2001/2008). *Introducing Translation Studies*, 2nd ed. Abingdon, UK: Routledge.

Naro, G. and Naro, M. W. (2014). Reducing Distance Between Characters, Narrator and Reader. Fictive Dialogue in Steinfest's *Nervöse Fische* and Its Translation into French. In S. M. Cadera and A. P. Pintarić, eds., *The Voices of Suspense and Their Translation in Thrillers*. Rodopi: Amsterdam, pp. 177–92.

No to Age Banding (n.d.). https://notoagebanding.org/.

Nodelman, P. (1988). *Words about Pictures*. Athens, Georgia: University of Georgia Press,

Nord, C. (1988). *Text Analysis in Translation*, 2nd ed. Amsterdam: Rodopi.

Nord, C. (1997). *Translating as a Purposeful Activity: Functionalist Approaches Explained*. Manchester: St. Jerome.

Nordic Noir. (2010). BBC 4 *Time Shift*. 21 December.

Oittinen, R. (1993). *I am Me – I am Other. On the Dialogics of Translating for Children*. Tampere, Finland: University of Tampere.

Oittinen, R. (2000). *Translating for Children*. New York: Garland.

Oittinen, R. (2018). Picturebooks and Translation. In B. Kümmerling-Meibauer, ed., *The Routledge Companion to Picturebooks*. Abingdon, UK: Routledge, pp. 463–70.

Owen, S. (2007). Genres in Motion. *PMLA*, 122(5), pp. 1389–93.

Palekar, S. (2017). Re-Mapping Translation. In B. J. Epstein and R. Gillett, eds., *Queer in Translation*. Abingdon, UK: Routledge, pp. 8–24.

Palmer, J. (1979). *Thrillers*. London: Edward Arnold.

Patton, C. and Sanchez-Eppler, B., eds. (2000). *Queer Diasporas*. Durham, NC: Duke University Press.

Peghinelli, A. (2012). Theatre Translation as Collaboration: A Case in Point in British Contemporary Drama. *Journal for Communication and Culture*, 2(1), pp. 20–30.

Porter, D. (1981). *The Pursuit of Crime*. New Haven: Yale University Press.

Reiβ, K. (1971/2000). Type, Kind and Individuality of Text: Decision Making in Translation. Transl. Susan Kitron. In L. Venuti, ed., *The Translation Studies Reader*. Abingdon, UK: Routledge, pp. 168–79.

Reynolds, K. (2011). *Children's Literature: A Very Short Introduction*. Oxford: Oxford University Press.

Robinson, L. S. (1983). Treason Our Text: Feminist Challenges to the Literary Canon. *Tulsa Studies in Women's Literature*, 2(1), pp. 83–98.

Romance Writers of America (RWA) (n.d.). About the Romance Genre. www.rwa.org/Online/Romance_Genre/About_Romance_Genre.aspx.

Rose, E. (2017). Revealing and Concealing the Masquerade of Translation and Gender: Double-Crossing the Test and the Body. In B. J. Epstein and R. Gillett, eds., *Queer in Translation*. Abingdon, UK: Routledge, pp. 37–50.

Rosenheim, Jr., E. W. (1961). *What Happens in Literature*. Chicago: University of Chicago Press.

Sánchez, J. L. A. (2014). 'Se So' Sparati a via Merulana': Achieving Linguistic Variation and Oral Discourse in the French and Spanish Versions of *Quer pasticciaccio brutto de via Merulana* (chapter 1). In S. M. Cadera and A. P. Pintarić, eds., *The Voices of Suspense and Their Translation in Thrillers*. Rodopi: Amsterdam, pp. 111–26.

Seago, K. (2014). Red Herrings and Other Misdirection in Translation. In S. M. Cadera and A. P. Pintarić, eds., *The Voices of Suspense and Their Translation in Thrillers*. Rodopi: Amsterdam, pp. 207–20.

Sedgwick, E. K. (1993). *Tendencies*. Durham, NC: Duke University Press.

Seed, D. (2011). *Science Fiction: A Very Short Introduction*. Oxford: Oxford University Press.

Shavit, Z. (2006). Translation of Children's Literature. In G. Lathey, ed., *The Translation of Children's Literature*. Clevedon: Multilingual Matters, pp. 25–40.

Sieghart, M. A. (2021). From Austen to Atwood, the Brontës to Booker Winners . . . Why Do So Few Men Read Books by Women? *The Guardian*, 10 July, p. 25.

Simon, S. (1996). *Gender in Translation: Cultural Identity and the Politics of Transmission*. Abingdon, UK: Routledge.

Škifić, S. and Petković, R. (2014). Stylistic and linguistic Creation of Suspense in Quentin Tarantino's Pulp Fiction and Reservoir Dogs. In S. M. Cadera and A. P. Pintarić, eds., *The Voices of Suspense and Their Translation in Thrillers*. Rodopi: Amsterdam, pp. 47–59.

Spivak, G. C. (1992/2004). The Politics of Translation. In L. Venuti, ed., *The Translation Studies Reader*, 2nd ed. Abingdon, UK: Routledge, pp. 369–88.

Strunk Jr., W. and White, E. B. (1935/2000). *The Elements of Style*, 4th ed. Boston: Allyn and Bacon.

Suh, J. C. (2002). Compounding Issues on the Translation of Drama/Theatre Texts. *Meta*, 47(1), pp. 51–7.

Sullivan, N. (2003/2011). *A Critical Introduction to Queer Theory*. Edinburgh: Edinburgh University Press.

Swedberg, S. (2021). Women's Literature. *Encyclopedia of the New American Nation*. www.encyclopedia.com/history/encyclopedias-almanacs-transcripts -and-maps/womens-literature.

UNICEF. (n.d.). The United Nations Convention on the Rights of the Child. www.unicef.org.uk/what-we-do/un-convention-child-rights/.

Van Coillie, J. and Verschueren, W. P. eds. (2006). *Children's Literature in Translation: Challenges and Strategies*. Manchester: St. Jerome.

Venuti, L. ed. (1995). *The Translator's Invisibility*. New York: Routledge.

Venuti, L. ed. (2004). *The Translation Studies Reader*, 2nd ed. Abingdon, UK: Routledge.

Vickery, A. (2020). Revaluing Memoir and Rebuilding Mothership in Maggie Nelson's *The Argonauts*. *Australian Literary Studies*, 35(1), pp. 1–15.

von Flotow, L. (1991). Feminist Translation: Contexts, Practices and Theories. *TTR*, 4(2), pp. 69–84.

von Flotow, L. (1997). *Translation and Gender: Translation in the Era of Feminism*. Manchester: St. Jerome.

von Flotow, L. ed. (2011). *Translating Women*. Ottawa: University of Ottawa Press.

Wallmach, K. (2006). Feminist Translation Strategies: Different or Derived? *Journal of Literary Studies*, 22(1–2), pp. 1–26.

Warwick Prize for Women in Translation (n.d.). https://warwick.ac.uk/fac/ cross_fac/womenintranslation/.

Wechsler, R. (1998). *Performing Without a Stage*. North Haven: Catbird Press.

Willett, E. A. R. (2016). Feminist Choices of Early Women Bible Translators. *Open Theology*, 2, pp. 400–4.

Wood, A. (2015). Making the Invisible Visible: Lesbian Romance Comics for Women. *Feminist Studies*, 41(2), pp. 293–334.

Woolf, V. (1929/2008). *A Room of One's Own*. Oxford: Oxford University Press.

Worthington, H. (2010). *Key Concepts in Crime Fiction*. London: Palgrave.

Wu, Y. (2020). Globalization, Science Fiction and the China Story: Translation, Dissemination and Reception of Liu Cixin's Works across the Globe. *Critical Arts*, 34(6), pp. 56–70.

Yoon, S. K. (2017). Deborah Smith's Infidelity: *The Vegetarian* as Feminist Translation. *Journal of Gender Studies*, 30(8), pp. 938–48, http://doi.org/10.1080/09589236.2020.1858039.

Yu, Z. (2017). Translation as Adaptation and Selection: A Feminist Case. *Perspectives*, 25(1), pp. 49–65, http://doi.org/10.1080/0907676X.2016.1197955.

Zatlin, P. (2006). *Theatrical Translation and Film Adaptation*. Clevedon: Multilingual Matters.

Acknowledgements

I owe much appreciation to Professor Emeritus Kirsten Malmkjær, the editor of this series, for her support, recommendations and enthusiasm. I am also grateful to the peer reviewers who provided useful suggestions and generous encouragement; their ideas have helped to make this book better.

I also want to extend my gratitude to all the students who have taken my module, Case Studies, at the University of East Anglia, as part of their MA programme in literary translation. In this class, we discuss issues of genre and style and try out different translation techniques, and I always find it fun, stimulating and enlightening. Thank you for all your contributions.

And, as always, I thank my wife, Fi, and our children, Esther and Tovah, for the joy and love they bring to my life every day.

Cambridge Elements ≡

Translation and Interpreting

Kirsten Malmkjær
University of Leicester

Kirsten Malmkjær is Professor Emeritus of Translation Studies at the University of Leicester. She has taught Translation Studies at the universities of Birmingham, Cambridge, Middlesex and Leicester and has written extensively on aspects of both the theory and practice of the discipline. *Translation and Creativity* (London: Routledge) was published in 2020 and *The Cambridge Handbook of Translation*, which she edited, was published in 2022. She is preparing a volume entitled *Introducing Translation* for the Cambridge Introductions to Language and Linguistics series.

Sabine Braun
University of Surrey

Sabine Braun is Professor of Translation Studies and Director of the Centre for Translation Studies at the University of Surrey. She is a world-leading expert on interpreting and on research into human and machine interaction in translation and interpreting, and holds an Expanding Excellence in England grant to investigate technology-assisted methods, modalities and socio-technological practices of translation and interpreting. She has written extensively on the theory and practice of interpreting, including *Videoconference and remote interpreting in criminal proceedings*, with J. Taylor, 2012; *Here or there: Research on interpreting via video link*, with J. Napier and R. Skinner, 2018. She is editing *Innovation in audio description research*, with K. Starr (2019), and guest-editing a special issue of the *Interpreter and Translator Trainer* with Russo (2020). She is a member of the AHRC Peer Review College.

About the Series
Elements in Translation and Interpreting present cutting edge studies on the theory, practice and pedagogy of translation and interpreting. The series also features work on machine learning and AI, and human-machine interaction, exploring how they relate to multilingual societies with varying communication and accessibility needs, as well as text-focussed research.

Cambridge Elements ≡

Translation and Interpreting

Elements in the Series

Translation and Genre
B. J. Woodstein

A full series listing is available at: www.cambridge.org/EITI

Printed in the United States
by Baker & Taylor Publisher Services